Body Language:
A Functional Approach to Gestures

Tzscheng-il Gahng

The Author

Tzscheng-il Gahng holds a Ph. D. in Applied Linguistics and a Master in Language Education. Since 1983, he has been Director / Professor of Inha University Language Center. He has pubished five books on communication skills, in addition to publishing numerous articles on language and communication.

Body Language:
A Functional Approach to Gestures

초판인쇄 2005 년 3월 1일 / 초판발행 2005년 3월 5 일
저자 강청일 / 발행인 서덕일 / 발행처 도서출판 문예림
출판등록 1962년 7월 12일 제 2-110호
주소 : 서울 광진구 군자동 195-21호 문예B/D 201호
전화 : 02-499-1281~2 / 팩스 : 02-499-1283
http://www.bookmoon.co.kr / E-mail : my1281@lycos.co.kr

· 잘못된 책은 구입하신 서점에서 교환하여 드립니다.

ISBN 89-7482-283-0 (13740)

contents

Acknowledgement ·· 4

Preface ··· 5

Introduction ·· 6

Perspectives ··· 10

Gestures as a Body Language ··············· 13

The Dictionary ·· 17

Bibliography ·· 120

ACKNOWLEDGEMENT

In the writing this book we have profitted immensely from the comments of many colleagues and visitors in the Communication Department at the University of Georgia. We would like to thank Doctor Rubin, and Doctor Joyce Gahng who has read various versions of this manuscript over a number of years. In addition, we wish to acknowledge the generous help of the following advisors, Earl, Margaret, Robyn, Tudor, Nancy , and Cornelia in providing us with material on their native languages, various aspects of which are compiled in this book.

Finally, we acknowledge the aid of Inha University Research Fund(2003) over a number of years for their generous financial support.

Tzscheng-il Gahng

Preface

A preface is where one makes excuses for all the books one might have written but did not. Our first excuse is that research in body language would not stand still while we were writing about it. In other words, this book is not, and really could not have been, an absolutely up-to-the minute, stop-press report of what is being said about gestures in the latest research journals. Some of the functional items of this book seem likely to be of lasting value. Other proposals we have included because they are there. Though their weaknesses are beginning to show through, they are a common heritage of nonverbal communication. In all revolutions a price is paid for progress. Seeing what was wrong with earlier moves is a large part of seeing how to get it right next time.

<u>Body Language: A Functional Approach to Gestures</u> is designed to be a basic text of body language — gesture courses for the future stage - and - screen stars.

Introduction

Communication takes many forms which are normally categorized into verbal and nonverbal components.

Almost everyone believe that it is the spoken word that is most important in communication. This perception is often not true. Research indicates that 93 percent of a person's attitude was communicated nonverbally and only 7 percent with words.

The first form of communnication we learn and use is nonverbal commuication.

Nonverbal behavior which is generated spontaneousely, and usually unconsciously, forms an integral part of daily communication. Although nonverbal behavior is not generally acknowledged, at least on a conscious level, its impact on total communication can be readily understood by examining the processes that lead to its generation and application. For example, nonverbal communication can be easily compared to something as common and normal as breathing.

Nonverbal behavior provides a necessary function, but one that is hardly ever acknowledged

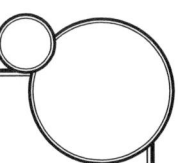

or planned.

Consider the implication of the reduction or loss of nonverbal communication channels and their impact on completion of the total communication message. For example, without sight a substantial portion of the message is lost. Further if sound is removed, the loss of the emotional component which is present in speech and which forms a vital link, inhibits completion of the total message. With the communication channels almost totally shut down, the listener is literally marooned into an uncertain communicative void.

Nonverbal communication is manifested in a variety of forms that are used simultaneously and are culture and gender specific.

Novnerbal behavior performs several functions, including its role in forming first impressions and its variety of possible relationships with verbal communication.

First impressions are based almost entirely upon nonverbal information, such as body shape, clothing, jewerly,eye contact, and facial expressions. The importance of nonverbal behavior does not stop with first impressions. Rather, nonverbal behavior is always an important part of the total communication process, whether verbal, nonverbal, or a combination of both.

In some situations, nonverbal behavior may be used to complement words. A complementing nonverbal message conveys the same meaning as the verbal message and , therefore, completes or supplements the verbal message. Making the gesture with the raised hand and using the index finger and the thumb to form a circle to show "O.K."while saying "The food is O.K."would also be a complementary verbal and nonverbal message.

Nonverbal communication may also accent words. An illustration of this would occur when a speaker inserts a pause before making a point in order to emphasize the significance of an idea.

Nonverbal messages also may be used to regulate both verbal and nonverbal communication.

Besides working in conjunction with spoken words, nonverbal communication can substitute for spoken words

Nonverbal communication can contradict spoken words.

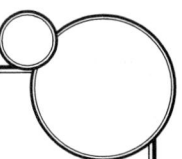

In addition to complementing, accenting, regulating, substituting, and contradicting verbal behavior, nonverbal communication has several characteristics that Rosenfeld (1997) pointed out.

Emotions and feelings are more accurately communicated nonverbally than verbally.

Nonverbal behaviors are not easily controlled consciously.

Nonverbal communication is more effective than vervbl communication for expressing messages in a confrontational manner.

Nonverbal behaviors indicate to both the speaker and the listener if the verbal message is understood and how it interpreted. The key to grasping the full content of the verbal message is the interpretation of the nonverbal underpinnings.

Perspectives

Pantomime is the very silent form of nonverbal communication in which the play developed by body language-body movement, facial expression, and gesture. In ancient Rome the pantomine was popular as an entertainment easily understood by the general masses.

The early silent moving pictures depended to a considerable extent on pantomime, aided by titles and explanatory legends: Charles Spencer(Charlie) Chaplin revealed himself as a great pantomimist

Ancient Greek and Roman scholars commented on what is today referred to as nonverbal communication. For example, Quintilian's Institutio Oratoria, which was written in the first century , is an important source of information on gesture. Tracing the history of fields including philosophy, anthropology, psychology, sociology, linguistics, psychiatry, dance, drama and speech, would no doubt reveal important antecedents for today's work.

One of the most influential pre-twentieth century works was Darwin's Expression of the Emotions in

Man and Animals in 1872. This work spawned the modern study of facial expressions and gestures.

In 1925, Kretschmer produced a book, Physigue and Character.

In 1940, Sheldon authored a book, The variety of Human Physique, In order to develop a catalogue of body types, Sheldon was permitted to photograph freshman students in the nude at Yale, Princeton, and other colleges. The students were told that it was a project involving posture,and thousands compiled, including the future U. S . President George Bush and the future first lady Hillary Rodham Clinton.

In 1941, Efron wrote a book, Gesture and Environment, which has become a classic. His work documented the important role of culture in shaping the use of gestures and body movement. At the time, Efron's thories were contrary to the belief of many (including Adolf Hitler)that people's behavior is not subject to much modification by changing context and environments.

Birdwhistell's Introduction to Kinesics appeared in 1952 and Hall's Silent Language in 1959. Davitz wrote The Communication of Emotional Meaning in

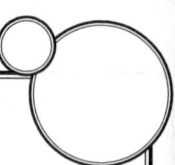

1964. Ekman's <u>Emotion in the Human Face</u>, in 1972; Mehabian's <u>Nonverbal Communication</u>, in 1972: Argyle's <u>Bodily Communication</u>, in 1975 were all attempts to bring together the growing literature on such research into a single volume.

During the 1980s and 1990s, nonverbal research continued to shift from studying non-interactive situations to studying interactive ones, from an emphasis on one culture to an emphasis on the intercultural and multicultural spheres. Leathers wrote <u>Successful Nonverbal Communication</u> in 1997, and Calloway—Thomas, Cooper and Blake published <u>Intercultural Commuication</u> in 1999.

Gestures as a Body Language

Gestures can be defined as "the use of interacting sets of visual communication systems and subsystems by communicators with the systematic encoding and decoding of nonverbal symbols and signs for the purposes of exchanging consensual meanings in specific communicative contexts."

Cultures that rely heavily on verbal language are referred as low context and those that put more stock in nonveral messages are known as high context. Anthropological studies show these cultures can be classified and placed on a continuum according to the emphasis placed either on verbal or nonverbal messages as the tools which convey meaning. At one end of the continuum are the German, French, Scandinavian, North American, and Engligh societies that believe the verbal message is extremely important. Conversely, the Japanese, Chinese, and Koreans believe that most meaning is found in the context in which people communicate. People from the latter group understand and interpret the conveyed contextual meaning without reverting to spoken words.

Indeed, the Korean language actually contains the word "nunchi", which literally means "being able to communicate through the eyes."

Body language is a communication through body movements. Body movements are motious such as gestures and postures. Postures, movements that involve our whole body, are useful for communicating general attitudes. Gestures are movements that carry meaning made by a particular parts of our body such as head, face,eye,arm, finger, leg, mouth, lips, and so on.

Universal emotions such as happiness, fear, and sadness are expressed in a similar nonverbal way throughout the world. However there are nonverbal differences across cultures that can be a source of confusion and misunderstanding for people from different cultures. For example, the "O.K." gesture in the American culture is a symbol for money in Korea and Japan, and a vulgar sexual threat in the Mediterranean area and in the Latin American countries. That's why the editors of a Brazilian newspaper enjoyed publishing a picture of an American President giving the "O.K." symbol with both hands.

Gestures have different meanings across cultures. Not all gestures are universal. Nonverbal language is closely linked to a person's cultural background. That is the very reason why we need to grasp new horizons of body language. In order to grasp the full scope in body language it is indispensable for us to understand gestures and postures expressing meaning and feeling without words.

The
Dictionary

ACCUSATION

Africa: Right hand extended, index pointing at the accused.

U.S.: Index fingers extended, pointing to both sides at once.

ACKNOWLEDGMENT

Netherlands: Applauded performer extends one arm upwards and outwards, and slowly moves it toward other performers, turning the extended hand in the same direction to indicate they are co-recipients of the applause.

U.S.: Sticking out hand as though to shake hands in acknowledgment of an introduction.

Venezuela, Brazil: Pronouncing and nodding as if to complete an introduction.

Spain: Right hand oscillates obliquely or semi-vertically in front of the nose.

U.S.: Slapping one across the anterior portion of the leg.

ADMONITION

Spain: Right hand oscillates obliquely or semi-vertically in front of the nose.

U.S.: Slapping one across the anterior portion of the leg.

AFFIRMATION

Arab: Dropping head downward and forward. Shaking of the head from side to side.

Bulgaria: Head inclined sideways left or right.

Colombia: Hands raised to level of head and clasped vigorously.

Eastern Europe: Palm upward, hand is moved in a slight curve upward and to the side.

Ethiopa: Throwing the head back, eyebrows raised. Jerking the head to the right shoulder in a sort of modified had shake.

England: Two rapid little nods.

France: Inclining the had and lifting it again.

France, U.S.: Thumb and forefinger of raised hand from a circle to indicate o.k.

Germany: Eyebrows lowered, eyes blinking.

Greece, Yugoslavia, Turkey, Iran: Shaking the head back and forth.

India: Head tossed backwards to indicate yes. Rocking the head slowly back and forth, side-to-side.

Japan: Hands repeatedly moved downward from height of throat.

Native American, U.S.: Raised index finger lowered.

Nepal: A short, sharp sideways jerk of the chin, which results in the whole head tipping from side to side once. Usually accompanied by a single grunt, glottal stop followed by long schwa.

Philippines: Eyebrows raised.

Russia: Holding up the thumb.

Spain: Index and thumb of left hand form right angle; indiex of right hand curls around left thumb, middle finger and thumb of right hand are snapped. Right hand clenched, index extended, forearm extended horizontally forward, elbow at waist, forearm waved rapidly vertically.

Universal: The handshake is a "masculine ritual of recognition and affirmation" serving to perpetuate male clubbiness and to exclude women from the club.

NEGATION

Africa: Quick jerk of left shoulder.

Arab: Blowing between the hands. Shaking head from side to side several times. Head raised, restricted movement of face, neck tending to remain stationary. Nodding of the head.

Balkans, Greece, Albania, Bulgaria, Turkey, Iran, Iraq, Syria, Palestine, Egypt: Chin raised in sudden movement, head back, eyelids half closed, eyebrows raised. Sometimes accompanied by click of the tongue.

Brazil: Hand raised to height of, and several inches in front of, speaker's mouth, fingers wagged.

Colombia: Thumb rests between chin and lower lip while fingers, extended, move from side to side. Index extended, moving from side to side.

France: Hand raised, palm outward, or simply the index raised, and shaken rapidly from side to side. Head shaken once or twice around vertical axis.

Greece: Raising hand, throwing head back, rolling eyes, raising eyebrows. Fingers of right hand together and rised, may consist of merely uncurling fingers or may involve raising hand as if to get attention.

Greece, Italy, Malta, Tunisia: Tossing the head back in negation.

India: A click with a toss of the head.

Italy: The "chin flick". Right hand is catapulted out from under the chin. Semi-rotating hand with thumb and index up. Palm open.

Italy, Sicily, Malta, Corfu, Sardinia: Backs of the fingers of one hand are flicked out from under the chin, as under indifference. Often accompanied the negative toss of the head.

Japan: Negation by gesture, apart from a blank face does not exist in the Japanese lexicon. Rarely one will see the right hand passed back and forth across the chest.

Jordan, Lebanon, Kuwait, Syria, Saudi Arabia: Hand in front of body, palm forward, hand shaken vigorously from side to side.

Latin America: Moving extended index of raised right

hand from side to side.

Lebanon: Head tilted back: accompanying "tsk" is optional; several times in a row means "too bad!"

Netherlands: Index extended, other fingers closed (palm forward) and wagged from side to side.

Portugal: Moving head from side to side rapidly.

Spain: Right hand clenched, index extended, forearm extended horizontally forward, elbow at waist, forearm waved rapidly back and forth horizontally in an arc of 90 degrees.

Spain, Latin America: With verbal expressions of inability, the bent arms are pushed forward, palms facing one another, then suddenly and sharply the arms are raised behind the body. Shoulders are shrugged while executing movement. Right hand raised, palm forward, fingers extended.

Syria: Biting nail of right thumb, then quickly protruding the hand.

U.S.: Arm bent, fingers closed, thumb extended and pointing forward. Hands, plam down, moved in opposite directions: both moving together in front of body, both moving apart (similar to the baseball "safe"). Shaking the head.

Venezuela: Index extended upwards from fist, palm outward, and waggeled from side to side with the forearm or wrist as fulcrum of the waggle. The waggled finger is at head height, but often to the side of the speaker's face.

ANNOYANCE

Argentina, Uruguay: Eyes rolled upwards, while head and eyebrows are slowly raised.

APPROVAL

Africa: Hand raised to level of face, fingers curled in, thumb extended vertically. Open hands raised above the head.

Central Asia: A person seeking approval or appreciation extends the open right hand, palm up. If approval is granted the other person strokes the extended hand with his palm.

Australia: The "thumbs up" gesture of approval is insulting.

Brazil: Pinching earlobe. To add emphasis to their appreciation, some Brazilians reach across the tope of the head to the opposite ear and grasp the earlobe.

Brazil, Portugal: Signal passage of an attractive woman by pinching the ear.

Colombia: Index touches skin below eye. Used frequently to refer to members of opposite sex. Extended index pointed at referent, then hand placed on chest. Fingers of one hand joined at tips and pressed against lips, then opened quickly and spread. Used more frequently by men. Can refer to a person or an object.

England: Double thumbs-up.

France: Thumb erect, corners of mouth drooping. Upturned thumb.

Germany: Nodding the head.

India: Smiling and wagging his head from side to side.

Italy: Tip of extended index placed against cheek and rotated as if screwing it into cheek. Particularly in approval of tase of food, but by extension also of anything good or beautiful.

Jordan: Slapping another man's palm with open palm - sign that person has done something done.

Jordan, Lebanon, Kuwait, Syria, Saudi Arabia, Egypt: Belching as a sign that one has enjoyed a meal.

Netherlands: Tips of index and thumb joined, placed to the lips and kissed, other fingers extended.

Portugal: Kissing the side of an index finger, then pinching an earlobe between the index and thumb compliments the hostess for her dinner.

Russia: Thumb extended upward from closed fist, fingers of other hand held above tip of extended thumb and rubbing tips together. Signals very strong approval. Right index taps right temple.

Spain: Clicking the tongue.

Syria, Egypt: Putting three fingers together.

Turkey: Hand raised, palm outward, fingers slowly bent under the thumb in a grasping motion, indicates that the gesturer approves of something.

U.S.: Thumb and index join to form a circle, palm facing outward. As the hand is raised and the fingers assume their position, it is briefly jerked forward and held still for a moment before being lowered. Hand closed, thumb erect. Hand raised, thumb and index forming a circle. Stamping feet at an athletic event. Patting the hair. Hand raised above head height, flat palm outward, slaps into flat palm of hand similarly held by another person. Nodding and clapping hands. The "high five" is also popular in the U.S.

DISAPPROVAL

Africa: Eyes opened wide and turned toward the person at fault. Lips pursed and pointed at the person at fault, accompanied by a fixed stare. Eyes opened wide, lower lip pushed forward in the direction of the person at fault.

Arab: Shaking head from side to side and clicking teeth simultaneously.

Europe, North America: Cheeks raised, direct stare, brows frowning, corners of mouth draw down. Whistling at a public performance.

U.S.: Nostrils are pinched between the thumb and forefinger with fingers 3,4, and 5 remaining lax and with the brows bilaterally and minimally raised. Hissing. Shaking the head with a grimace. Also, a dead-pan look.

ADMIRATION

Africa: Arms akimbo, hands at waist. Hands gently touch one's hair several times in admiration of someone's hairstyle. Both hands pass gently over the face and follow the contours of the face of a beautiful woman.

Arab: Grasping one's beard in admiration of a pretty woman.

Argentina, Uruguay: Tips of thumb and index joined, other fingers half open, make 45 degree rotary movement against the corresponding cheek, almost always accompanied by a click of the tongue.

Brazil: Placing an imaginary telescope to one's eye in admiration of a pretty woman. Thumbnail rapidly bitten by incisors indicates admiration for a culinary performance.

Colombia: With palms facing each other, hands move downward from shoulder-level to hip-level, exaggerating an attractive female figure.

Europe, North America: Head forward, eyebrows raised, slight smile raising cheeks. Biting lower lip, eyebrows raised, lips and cheeks extended as in laugh.

France: Placing thumb and index together to form a circle. Mouth firm, somewhat drooped, thumb of right hand erect and pushed forward as if pushing thumbtack, signifying "first class." Kissing fingertips in admiration of a pretty woman.

Germany: Clapping hands. Expressing admiration by

making a "wolf whistle."

Greece: Stroking one's cheek in admiration for a pretty woman.

Italy: Tip of index pressed into cheek while whistling ? admiration for a pretty woman. Index pulls down lower eyelid, while the other hand indicates object of admiration. Hand shaken as if burnt. Particularly signifies admiration of feminine beauty.

Jordan, Lebanon, Syria: Tips of right index, middle finger and thumb held in pear-shaped configuration and kissed while bowing slightly forward, then the head is flicked up.

Lebanon, Syria: Tip of right index run down the cheek of a woman— a compliment.

Libya: Twisting tip of forefinger into check, when speaking to a beautiful woman. Thumb extended from right fist, but not moving it: item referred to is best.

Netherlands: Hand slightly extended, palm up, slightly cupped and jerked slightly upwards while one eye winks at a male companion. A vulgar male gesture of erotic admiration for a female body. Erotic admiration is expressed by quickly extruding and withdrawing the tongue.

Russia: Both hands grasp head at or above temples.

Spain: Index and thumb of right hand are placed respectively above and below the eye as if to make the eye larger. Fingertips of right hand united and brough to the lips. To show greater admiration, nails of the three united fingertips are kissed and opened hand is quickly drawn back from the lips. Clicking the tongue.

Uruguay: Tips of fingers of one hand joined in pear-shaped configuration touch lips gently, quickly move away while lips make kissing sound.

U.S.: Lifting eyebrows in admiration of a pretty girl. Creating curves in the air with his hands.

ADORATION

Middle East: Raising the hand.

South Africa: Spitting in the direction of a deity.

AFFECTION

Asia: Kissing an intimate sexual act not permissible in public.

Argentina: Joined fingers are kissed, hand is opened, palm upward, at level of mouth, and the imaginary kiss is blown toward the person intended.

Argentina, Uruguay: Joined fingers of both hands are kissed, then arms extended to both sides. Commonly used with actresses and boxers.

Bolivia: Touching or tapping someone lightly for whom affection is felt.

Colombia: Kissing palm of own hand, then extending hand. Used to express gesture when people are at a distance.

Colombia, U.S.: Tongue protrudes slightly and moves

slowly along lips. Primarily used by male adolescents. Request for a kiss.

Egypt, Lebanon, Jordan, Syria, Saudi Arabia: Pinching right cheek of another person with tips of right index and thumb.

France: Taking someone by the neck or the shoulders, then putting the lips on his forehead, or on his cheeks, or on his lips.

Germany: Slapped affectionately on the back. Pinching on the cheek by index and middle finger. Hands laid upon someone's head in blessing.

Greece: Girls kiss one another on the eyes while holding the other's ears.

Jordan, Syria, Lebanon: Flicking the underside of a woman's chin with the tip opf right index, considered conciliatory.

Mongolia: Nose laid against cheek of beloved taking a deep breath, eyes closed, then lips make sound of a kiss without touching the cheek.

Netherlands: Pursing the lips, sometimes also making the sound of a kiss, toward someone at some distance indicates affection; similar to throwing a kiss.

Saudi Arabia: Hands moved up the sides of the chest so that thumbs hit undersides of lapels; head is shaken slightly. Symbolizes unrequited love.

U.S.: Fingertips of right hand kissed and thrown forward.

AGREEMENT

Africa: Eyebrows rapidly raised and lowered.

England: Linking little fingers of right hands and shaking them up and down, occasionally repeating a warning — making a bargain.

Ethiopia: Raising eyebrows and throwing head back.

Europe, Brazil: The palm of the right hand slaps against the palm of the person spoken to, followed by an energetic handshake.

France: Palm of right hand is touched to the palm of the right hand of the partner, then the right hand is presented to be touched by the palm of the partner's right hand. Signifies mutual agreement concerning a transaction.

Germany: Raising the hand. Handclasp, a bystander separates the hands by bringing the edge of his right hand down upon the clasped hands, signifying the conclusion of a bargain.

India: At the conclusion of an agreement, both parties break a straw between them.

Italy: Indexes of both hands extended, other fingers lightly closed. Tips of indexes touch and separate repeatedly.

Middle East: The two indexes, palm of hands down, are rubbed together.

U.S.: Right hand raised, palm laid in the palm of the raised right hand of the partner.

DISAGREEMENT

Africa: One eye rapidly closed, mouth twisted to the side, head slightly inclinded. Eyes fixing the person with whom the gesturer disagrees, eyebrows drawn together. Tip of index placed on mouth by pointing at it from the front. Right hand open, placed on mouth, then brought forward until arm is extended in the direction of person with whom gesturer is speaking.

Colombia: Forearm at right angle to upper arm, fist clenched and moved back and forth several times; considered impolite. Indexes pointed at each other and moved repeatedly apart and together.

England: Linking thumbs, shaking them up and down, accompanied by a verbal formula.

Europe, North America: Arms crossed over chest ? a defensive posture or an expression of disagreement. One corner of mouth smiling, the other drawn down, eyelids drooping.

Lebanon, Saudi Arabia: Hands moved up from waist level with palms up.

Spain: Expressions of contrast may be accompanied by bent arms at shoulder level or higher, palms facing each other.

Spain, Latin America: Twisting cupped hands away from the speaker at chest level, concluding with palms facing the listener. Tight fists, palms down, are brought toward each other. May be repeated. When accompanying verbal expressions suggest confrontation, fingers do not touch, but stop a few inches from one another.

AMAZEMENT

Europe: Placing the palm on either the cheek or behind the ear. Palm placed behind the ear.

Europe, North America: Eyebrows raised, mouth open, should raised.

France: Index of right hand placed alongside of nose, mouth slightly open, eyes wide open.

Spain, Latin America: Shaking loosely held fingers of slightly cupped hand in front of the speaker or at the side at waist-level.

Universal: Rolling the eyes.

ANGER

Africa: Arms extended slightly to the side, hands open, body inclined toward the object of one's anger. Arms akimbo, hands at waist. Arms lowered and spread slightly to the side, hands open. Stamping the right foot.

Brazil: Biting fingertips.

Colombia: Fist moved from left to right several times at approximate chin level. Fists held together and twisted as if wringing cloth. Clenched fists held so that knuckles face downward, forearms extended in front parallel to ground; fists make short, sharp downward and upward motion.

England: Biting one's thumb.

Europe: Eyes wide open, clenched teeth, lips pulled back so that teeth are visible.

Europe, North America: Fists clenched in front, eyes staring, eyebrows drawn down. Hands hanging at side and clenched. Hands vertically extended, palms facing out, fingers separated and hooked.

Germany: Chewing on one's moustache.

Latin America: The tips of the fingers are struck together. Tapping floor with the foot. Knuckles of both hands rubbed together. Right fist rubbed on the extended left palm. Beating the thighs with fists. Biting one's lips to check the flow of words.

Lebanon, Syria: Both fists clenched at waist level, thumbs extended in opposite direction.

Lebanon, Syria: Middle East: The little fingers are hooked together and then released. This is repeated two or three times.

Netherlands: Striking fist into palm.

Portugal: Abdomen pushed out toward someone facing one. If adversary is small, he may be pushed with abdomen. Standing up. When angry person feels superior to the other, he will approach, staring, grab the other by lapel or arm, or touch his face and fingers. Equal adversaries grab each other.

Saudi Arabia: Middle finger held down with thumb,

other fingers extended, hand shaken at someone. Biting lower lip with upper teeth and shaking head from side to side.

Saudi Arabia, Syria: Right index extended from fist, pointing upwards, eyes looking upwards; anger or swearing an oath.

Spain, Latin America: Accompanying expression of anger, raising arm vertically from neutral position to near touching the head, then dropping it to original position. Both arms extended toward the offender, fingers extended, palms parallel, hands shaking vigorously at the side of the listener's face. Striking the open palm of one hand with the closed fist of the other hand.

Syria: Twisting one side of face.

Universal: Red face, contraction of cheek, mouth, chin, or brow muscles.

U.S.: Kicking. Mouth drawn down and upper face pulled into a tight frown. Gritting one's teeth as indication of extreme anger or rage.

APOLOGY

Japan: Silently fall to knees and slowly bringing foreheads to the floor.

Netherlands: Lower arms raised sideways so that open hands, palm up, are at height of the shoulders. Suddenly placing a hand over one's mouth is the same as an apology for something one has said.

Saudi Arabia: Biting middle joint of right index with heel of hand pointing forward, hand closed. Kissing the top of another man's head after quarreling. Kissing the nose of a person with whom one has fought.

U.S.: Arms spread open and hands held open. Holding a fixed stare and shaking the head.

APPRECIATION

France, Italy, Spain, Latin America: Kissing the tips of one's fingers.

Italy, Asia: Picking teeth with toothpick in public after a meal.

Netherlands: Circular movement of flat hand on abdomen with happy expression indicating enjoyment of meal.

U.S.: Patting abdomen. Two hands curved in the air to suggest an attractive female shape may express appreciation or sensuousness. Smacking the lips after a meal. Also, whistling at a public performance is usually a sign of approval.

ASTONISHMENT

Africa: Left elbow rests on the right forearm and little finger of the left hand touches the mouth. Arms akimbo, hands on hips. Chin drops, open mouth utters cry. With a thoughtful expression, the thumb and index pinch the lower lip. Open right taps lightly on the open mouth.

U.S.: Suddenly covering the mouth.

ATTENTION

Africa: Fingers of right hand grasp earlobe and shake it. Elbow gives a neighboring person a blow in the side to indicate "pay attention." One eye rapidly closed, mouth twisted to the side, head slightly inclined. Index extended forward and slowly moved up and down. Hand raised and index extended upward. Right index pointing upward and moving back and forth, while left hand is pointed in the direction of danger. Open right hand raised to level of mouth, threating to slap someone.

Argentina, Uruguay: Eyes directed at the person whose attention is sought, eyebrows raised, head rapidly raised.

Asia: Extended arm-sign of animation and action. During excitement and discussion it is an understood prelude to speech, implying possession of something that ought to be heard.

Austria: Raising arm with index and middle finger extended.

Colombia: Index pointed to eye, then to object to which attention is to be directed. If no such object, the index is merely pointed at the eye. Clapping to call waiter. Hand extended to get teacher's attention. Tapping table top with ring or glass, or tapping glass or cup with another object to get waiter's attention. Short hiss to call waiter.

Colombia, U.S.: Neighbor is nudged with elbow. Proper only with close friends. Hand extended with fingers together. Hand raised, finger extended.

England: Laying a hand on shoulder. Tapping on the desk with a pencil, followed by clearing throat.

Europe, North America: Head to one side, gaze directly forward, eyebrows raised, smile. Head to one side, eyes turned to the side. Listening.

France: Raising arm with index extended. Looking at a person while closing one eye. Snapping thumb against middle finger or ringfinger. The index finger used as a warning and in an argument by thrusting it up and holding it rigid beneath the conversation partner's nose signaling caution.

Germany: Pursing lips

Italy: Index and thum of one hand brough to the cheeks to draw attention to whatever expression the face makes.

Japan: Eyes closed, head nodding slightly shows attentiveness. Clapping hands to call attention of spirits, awaken and call souls of ancestors during worship.

Netherlands: Extended index shaken back and forth.

Russia: Snapping the fourth finger and thumb of the right hand.

U.S.: Hand cupped behind ear, indicating that one is giving attention. Raising hand to get waiter's attention. Waving hand from side to side to get teacher's attention. Rising and banging on a water glass with a spoon. Head and neck cocked to the right. Kicking legs in desire for attention.

Vietnam: When someone is talking, fold arms against body and demonstrate complete attention by displaying inactive hands.

AVARICE

Africa: Right hand slightly extended forward, palm up, fingers closed on palm.

Argentina, Uruguay: Fist closed, forearm raised, elbow thrust forward and struck by palm of other hand; or hitting a tabletop with the elbow when seated at a table.

Chile, Argentina: Arm raised to chest height, fist closed.

Colombia: Cupped hand, or fist, strikes elbow several times in succession. Tapping an elbow with the other hand to indicate the person is "cheap."

Europe, North America: Hands extended horizontally, fingers separated and hooked.

Latin America: Touching table with the elbow to signify being thrifty. Left forearm held up with fist clenched, the right palm strikes the left elbow, or the left elbow strikes any surface, and the clenched fist opens.

Mexico: Lifting forearm vertically and hitting bottom of elbow with palm of other hand is an insult.

Spain: Tips of thumb and index of the right hand joined, accompanied by the exclamation "not even this much." Left fist raised, right hits under left elbow, simultaneously the fingers of the left fist open.

U.S.: Rubbing the thumb over the tips of the first two fingers.

AMUSEMENT

Netherlands: Winking to demonstrate amusement. Index of each hand placed on corners of mouth, pulling lips in imitation of a smile, indicates that one is not amused.

Spain: Extended and rigid arm raised from position of rest at side of body to approximate level of shoulder; normally raised to side rather than front. Rare among women.

ANTICIPATION

Africa: Flat right hand slaps bottom of bent left elbow to indicate that enjoyment is forthcoming.

Colombia: Tongue extended approximately one-fourth inch moving slowly along lips; eyes widen.

France, U.S.: Right palm rubbed rapidly over

horizontally extended left palm; joyful face; shoulders sometimes hunched.

U.S.: Hands palm to palm or clasped in front of body.

ANTIPATHY

Italy: Head is thrown back on seeing or hearing something unpleasant.

U.S.: Hand extended, palms facing outward.

ANXIETY

England: Fingers pressed against the lips.

Germany: Biting nails.

U.S.: Hands twisted together in a wringing motion.

APPLAUSE

Colombia: Thumbnails tapping against one another, one hand held above the other.

Europe: Whistling as a sign of derision in a situation in which one would normally applaud.

Germany: Clapping hands.

Panama: Ironic applause.

Russia: Group tosses a person in the air several times.

U.S.: Clapping hands together and whistling as sign of approval.

ARROGANCE

Europe: Raising the hand, which is drawn slightly to the rear, lips closed, stiff posture.

Europe, North America: Head turned and thrown back.

Portugal: Head raised with a certain delay.

Russia: Open hands, held in front of stomach, joined by interlaced fingers, palms facing up, thumbs rotating around each other. Used almost exclusively by adults to indicate that someone is arrogant or conceited.

APPROACH

Asia, Spain: Clapping hands.

Britain, Netherlands, Scandinavia, Germany, Austria, Belgium, France: Beckoning with the palm up.

Colombia: Snapping fingers to summon waiter. Writing in the air with an imaginary pen or pencil to intended the act of computing the check is a movement observed in restaurants to call for the check. Index finger bent toward gesticulator, palm up. Fingers together or moving separately, usually beginning with the smallest; the latter primarily used by women.

Eastern Mediterranean: Fingers repeatedly straightened and bent, palm up.

Europe: Palm up, fingers repeatedly straightened and bent. Open hand waved laterally could be considered signaling 'no'. Head tossed up and back in a short jerk.

Europe, North America: Hand raised, palm inwards at level of face, arm half bent, tips of fingers moved inward.

France: Index crooked, moving repeatedly toward gesturer.

Germany: Raising the arm and moving it toward oneself in a wave - waving the person to approach.

Hong Kong, Indonesia, Australia, Yugoslavia: Palm up, index extended and repeatedly bent; used for calling animals.

India: Hand raised, palm outwards, fingers moved downwards and toward palm; beckoning.

Indonesia: Beckoning with the index is only used to call animals; it is considered insulting if used to people, but sometimes used to beckon prostitutes.

Iran, Lebanon, China, Fiji, India, Japan, Philippines, Singapore, Taiwan, Thailand, Argentina, Bolivia, Colombia, Guatemala, Mexico, Puerto Rico: Beckoning generally takes the form of holding the hand palm down and curling the fingers in a scratching motion.

Italy: Arm extended, palm down, four fingers extended, then repeatedly folded down to touch palm. Both forms (palm up and palm down). Hand flapped, palm down. Palm down, fingers repeatedly straightened and bent.

Italy, Greece: Palm-down beckoning gesture can be confused with palm-down farewell gesture in which the fingers are waggled up and down; whereas in the beckoning gesture, they make a scratching motion.

Italy, North Africa: Palm down, fingers closed, index repeatedly straightened and bent.

Japan: Extended index is considered rude.

Jordan, Lebanon, Saudi Arabia, Syria: Right hand held up, palm down, then moved several times in slightly clawing motion.

Malaysia: Beckoning by repeatedly bending the index, palm up, is used only for calling animals.

Malta, Spain, Tunisia, Turkey, Corfu, Sicily, Sardinia: Palm-down beckoning is common.

Netherlands: Index pointing downward, hand moved forward from should height to the level of the waist signifying "come, come here."

Saudi Arabia: Man simultaneously wrinkles his nose and one cheek to a woman if he wants her to come to him. Snapping index and thumb; call for someone to approach.

Saudi Arabia, Lebanon: Clap hands once or twice to signal the waiter to come.

Spain: Calling animals, one snaps middle finger against thumb, palm facing down. Arm and hand extended in front of chest, palm down, fingers lowered and raised repeatedly.

Spain, Portugal, Morocco, Turkey, Arab countries, Greece: Greeting with palm down, all fingers repeatedly straightened and bent.

U.S.: Spreading the arms upon greeting. Holding up one finger and shouting when summoning a taxi. Hand raised, index extended to call a taxi. Raising hand with index extended, or the open hand, waved slightly laterally, about head high. Drawing in flat of hand, palm toward gesturer. Head held high and protruding forward; hands at waist level, palms up, fingers meeting, hand slightly curled.

Vietnam: One finger is used to beckon to animals, four fingers to beckon to people.

ASSISTANCE

Colombia: Arm and hand extended, palm facing down; fingers, hand or arm may be moved up and down.

Saudi Arabia: Lightly putting one's heart with right palm indicates need for assistance.

Spain, Latin America: Index of one hand raised upward in a series of spirals alongside the body and head, together with references to divine wisdom or intervention.

U.S.: Request for a ride (hitchhiking): forward swing of the forearms, bent at the elbow and held upright or horizontal with thumb extended.

ASSURANCE

Africa: Hand raised to the shoulder level, tips of index and thumb joined, forming a circle; other fingers extended.

Europe, North America: Head raised, brows lowered, firm glance.

India: All fingers spread out, thumb curled up.

Netherlands: Tip of index and middle finger placed on closed eyelids, accompanied by an expression such as "May I go blind if this is not true."

Russia: Tip of thumb placed at the edge of the upper front teeth and flicked out. Sometimes combined with the throat-cutting gesture.

AWARENESS

England, France: Awareness of an attempt to wit saying: "You can't fool me."

France: Palm of hand struck against forehead. Fingers of both hands on both sides of forehead.

Italy, France: To reflect awareness of a secret: index touches lower lid of the right eye, sometimes pulls it down a little.

Spain: Hitting one's head at the side with flat right hand to express sudden awareness.

BEGINNING

Japan: Forming a circle with thumb and forefinger signifies begging for money.

South Africa: Holding out two cupped hands abutting at the edge of their palms.

BETTING

Africa: Each partner takes one end of a leaf in the right hand and pulls, so that the leaf tears. Little finger of right hand hooked into little finger of partner's right hand or each partner raises right hand above his head and clicks his fingers.

Colombia: Licking thumb and pressing it against the thumb of a disbeliever who has also licked his thumb signifies "you want to bet?" Wetting thumb and holding it up, shouting "I bet you." Bettors link little fingers of one hand. Sometimes one strikes linked fingers with free hand.

Germany: Hand clasp.

Scotland: Two people lick their thumbs and say "Bets," and press their thumbs together to signify that they accept a bet. If one person does not lick the thumb or touch the other's, it signifies that a proposed bet is not accepted.

BLESSING

Brazil: Arm extended to saints on altar, then one kisses one's own hand, in asking for, and receiving a blessing.

Cambodia: Thumb and index united, other fingers extended. Throwing water on someone as a form of wishing them good luck at the customary New Year's blessing.

Czech Republic: Third finger crosses index.

Italy, Portugal, Brazil: On completing the Sign of the Cross, kissing thumbnail.

Russia: Index, middle finger, and thumb are joined lightly at the tips, touching first the forehead, then the breast, then the right and left shoulders.

Tunisia: Paying respects to tombs of holy men, kissing back of the hand as it pointed the tombs out.

BODY DISTANCE

Latins and Middle Easterners: Usually quite close, less than twelve inches.

North America: Normally stand approximately thirty inches, about an arm's length, apart from one another.

Russia: Male normally maintain a distance of six to ten inches apart. In rural areas, this distance is reduced. Women avoid creating any distance between each other, often touching arms or hands while sitting closely side by side. Women of all ages customarily stroll arm in arm.

BOREDOM

Africa: Hands raised to chest height, palm down, fingers slightly curved, are suddenly moved forward. Hands placed at the back of the head while one stretches and yawns.

Argentina, Uruguay: Flat hand approximately twenty centimeters below the chin, palm down, as if supporting a beard.

Colombia, U.S.: Yaw, deliberate or involuntary. If deliberate, it is a signal that one wants to leave.

Europe, North America: Lowering and drawing together of the eyebrows, jaws contracted, corners of mouth drawn down.

Europe, U.S.: Yawning indicates tiredness or boredom, impolite in public if one does not cover the mouth.

France: Hand rubbed against cheek. Back of fingers of one hand lightly travel up and down over the chin. Fingers of one hand are interlaced with those of the other, and the two thumbs continuously turn around each other.

France, Brazil: Rotating thumbs around each other indicates boredom or tranquility.

Italy: Stroking an imaginary beard. Four fingers of right hand crossed in four fingers of left, rotating thumbs, around each other, turning and changing their direction.

Netherlands: Drawing the hand downward from the chin as if stroking a beard. To indicate that the joke that someone is telling is very old, one puts hand under chin, palm up as if to hold own beard, and then lowers it to indicate that the joke has a long beard.

Russia: Open hands, held in front of stomach, joined by interlacing fingers, palms facing upward, thumbs turning around each other.

U.S.: Fingers drum rhythmically on a surface, usually beginning with the little finger and moving to thumb.

CALM

Africa: Arms slightly raised, hands at shoulder height, palms outward, and repeatedly and slowly moved slightly downward; hands moved slightly back and forth. Tapping lightly by hand on opposite arm.

Netherlands: Arms slightly raised, hands at shoulder height, palms outward, and repeatedly and slowly moved slightly downward.

Russia: Fingers spread, arms slowly pulled back and repeated until excitement subsides.

Saudi Arabia: Flip hand near mouth and simultaneously make a clicking sound with tongue and teeth to indicate that a person is not to worry.

Spain, Latin America: Outstretched hands, palms down,

pushed toward the floor, indicate request for calmness.

Universal: Folding of hands indicates calmness.

CARELESSNESS

Spain: Twisting the open hand back and forth, fingers together, palm may face down.

CHALLENGE

Africa: Fist, thumb on top, raised to height of chest.

Brazil: Twisting the mustache.

Europe, North America: Head turned and thrown back.

Indonesia: Hands on hips with arms akimbo.

Lebanon, Saudi Arabia: Gently grazing another person's chin with tip of right index indicates a threat or challenge.

Portugal: Head lifted rapidly. Moving head from side to side repeatedly and slowly.

Syria, Saudi Arabia: Knocking sand from a boy's hand by another boy indicates a challenge or acceptance of a challenge to fight.

CLEVERNESS

France: Tapping the side of the nose with a finger. Winking and tapping the side of the nose. Swaggering while walking.

Italy: Index drawn down the outer corner of the eye.

Netherlands: Index draws down the lower lid of the eye.

Russia: Right hand, loosely open, palm up, held just below the waist, then swings to the genital area and away to the right.

Spain: Right index pulls down right lower eyelid indicating that someone is clever, or that one is clever enough to see through someone else's intentions.

Spain, Latin America: Pointing to the forehead with the index of one hand or tapping forehead with fingers of one hand.

U.S.: Tapping side of the nose.

COLDNESS

Africa: Arms crossed on check, body slightly inclined forward. Hands, palm against palm, placed between legs. Both hands placed on nape of the neck indicates that the gesturer is either sick or cold. Open right hand passes several times up and down the throat.

Colombia: Each hand grasps opposite upper arm, shoulders hunched.

Spain: Rubbing hand together vigorously.

U.S.: Fists placed near shoulder and shaking.

COMMAND

France: Snapping fingers and pointing.

Netherlands: Looking directly at someone, eyebrows raised, index pointing at him, signals "Come here."

COMPLICITY

England, Italy: Index finger placed along the nose and tapping it gently several times.

Europe, North America: Winking with one eyelid.

France: Tapping the side of the nose. Gesture also signifies a necessity for alertness or cleverness.

Germany: Placing his middle finger on the left eyelid and pulling it down.

Italy: Tapping the nose as a friendly warning.

U.S.: Placing index finger across the lips and winking ludicrously. Laying a finger beside the nose.

CONCENTRATION

Argentina, Uruguay: Extended index placed with tip against temple. Tip of extended index placed against tip of nose, pushing it up slightly.

Brazil: Lips pressed together.

Buddhist: Fixing one's eyes in the distance without perceiving any object.

Egypt, Jordan, Lebanon, Kuwait, Saudi Arabia, Syria: Tip of right or left index scratches back of one's head which indicates concentration or possibly veracity of someone's statement.

Europe, North America: Placing tongue in cheek. Plucking of beard or stroking of chin. Fixed look, head forward.

France: Putting together tips of five fingers to one point.

Japan: Gaze directed at the sun while praying.

Netherlands: Thumbs placed along nose, other fingers curled around eyes in imitation of binoculars indicates reflection or concentration on something. Making the victory sign.

Russia: Narrowing the eyes.

U.S.: Supporting face with hands. Scratching forehead. Index laid on brow, head lowered. Stroking beard, head, and moustache. Pursing lips. Eyes steady and directly forward, one hand in pocket. Arms raised to level of head, hands clasped.

CONFUSION

Africa: Open right hand is placed vertically in front of face.

Europe, North America: Head bowed, crosswise and double movement of the eyebrows, lips taut, weight of body on backward foot.

Netherlands: Open hand raised, vertically to approximately eye level, then moved past the face and downwards, gradually closing as it moves. The gesture indicates that the gesturer thinks someone is temporarily confused. Same gesture can also be a compliment.

Portugal: Hiding face in hands. Lowering head. Turning head aside.

: **A Functional Approach to Gestures**

CONGRATULATION

England: Shaking hands.

Netherlands: Shaking hands and looking pointedly at the person one is congratulating. Slapping someone on the shoulder.

U.S.: Clinking glasses while drinking a toast.

CONSOLATION

Netherlands: Wiggling one's thumb in front of the eyes of someone who is sad.

Universal: Holding tightly or picking up a child.

U.S.: Placing the hand on someone's shoulder to signify moral support or comfort.

CONTEMPLATION

U.S.: Thumb and index each stroking down one side of the face.

CONTEMPT

Arab: Right thumbnail is placed under tip of upper front teeth, then withdrawn rapidly, creating a noise.

Brazil: Striking one's buttocks.

Buddhist: Closing of eyes during prayer not only aids concentration, but signifies contempt of surroundings.

England: Turning up one's nose.

France: Tips of fingers passed rapidly from back to front three or four times under the chin. The "chin flick" which is brushing the fingernails of one hand under the chin and then flicking the fingers outward. Place the right thumbnail inside the upper front teeth; bring the thumb and enclosed fist forward in a sharp, throwing motion. While making this gesture sometimes a hissing noise is made.

Fist of right hand is clenched, thumbnail inserted under upper front teeth, then snapped forward, face scornful. Rapid shrugging of shoulders once or twice, often accompanied by sighs and raising of eyes to sky.

Germany: Thumb protruded between clenched index and middle or middle and ring fingers.

India: Monks turn their backs to the world in order to separate themselves from it. Open palm, fingers radiating from it and bent slightly back.

Italy: Tips of fingers rubbed together. Index, extended, is raised one or twice.

Mexico: Both hands form a circle approximately ten to thirty centimeters in diameter, indicating the size of anal area of the person despised.

Saudi Arabia: Hand extended, fingers in shape of claws, moved back and forth several times. Holding out left hand, palm forward, in front of face, then hitting the back of it lightly with palm of right hand.

Spain: Alternately winking with left and right eye, lips stretched laterally, tip of tongue protruded. Upward snub of nose executed by throwing head upward and sideward.

U.S.: Arm moved downward and to one side away from the body with a flick of the wrist. Thrusting out the middle finger. Middle finger of either hand extended, fist clenched, or at least the other fingers bent.

COUNTING

Africa: Thumb of left hand raised, then the tip of the right index ticks off in succession the left thumb, index, etc.: first, second, etc. Fingers of left hand extended and raised, index of right hand ticks off in succession the little finger of the left, then the ring finger, etc: one, two, etc.

Europe, North America: Thumb extended to represent "one." Index of one hand points to the middle of the index of the other hand to represent "one-half."

France: Thumb, index, middle finger of left hand are successively grasped by right. Right hand raised to the height of the face, clinched fist, thumb raised to represent "one." Thumb and index extended for two. Thumb, index, and middle finger extended for three. Right hand raised to the height of the face, fingers extended, left hand raised, thumb and index extended for seven. Both hands raised to the height of face, all fingers extended to represent ten. Both hands raised to the height of the face, fingers extended, then both hands closed to fists and the right thumb extended for eleven. Clasping successively with the right hand the thumb, the index, and the middle finger of the left hand.

Japan: Index raised to represent "one." Thumb raised for five. Thumb and index extended for six.

Kuwait, Iraq, Syria, Saudi Arabia: Throwing stones of dates over shoulder while eating dates: each stone indicates a camel acquired in a raid.

Latin America: Thumb and fingers of one hand raised while simultaneously saying the numbers.

Russia: Count beginning with the little finger, which is bent on the count of one. Successive fingers are bent as one counts, the thumb remaining upright until the count of five. The position of the thumb is distinguished from the gesture of approval by holding it upright, but extended outward when counting. The left hand may hold the right while counting.

Spain: Both hands used in counting, beginning the count with the small finger and separating each finger from the others.

CRAZY

Italy: Flat hand, palm down, extended to the forehead in the form of a military salute which can mean "you're crazy."

Netherlands: Palm or hand placed on someone's forehead. Snatching at an imaginary fly in front of the gesturer's face indicates that someone is crazy.

CUNNING

Argentina, Uruguay: Tip of index placed against side of nose, closing one nostril, while sniffing through the other, signifies discovery or understanding of something concealed.

England: Tapping the side of the nose with the index finger.

Europe: Lowered eyelids, raised eyebrows, face muscles tense, lips lightly closed.

France: Tilting the head and laying a finger along the side of the nose.

Italy: Index touches cheekbone; gesture accompanied by slight nod. Tapping the side of the nose.

Mexico: Fist clenched, index and little finger extended used to indicate shyness, cunning, maliciousness, perverseness. In this situation, the hand is not held near the forehead.

CUROSITY

Italy: Nostrils drawing in air abruptly and repeatedly. Head forward, moving from right to left, eyes lively, lips pursed. Imitating sniffing dog.

Puerto Rico: Wiggling the nose.

Body Language

DANGER

Africa: Index of right hand points upward and moves back and forth while left hand indicates direction of the danger. Head back, closed right hand raised to height of head.

Russia: Index and middle finger spread apart, forming a "V" and held with tips against the throat at the Adam's apple; a metaphor for having a pitchfork held at one's throat. Index and middle finger of right hand extended and placed on left shoulder.

DEATH

Africa: Body straight, arms down the side, head slightly inclined backwards. Arms raised and thrown backward while body leans backward to indicate the death of an animal. Extending arms sideways, hands open, palm down, whle body moves as if collapsing.

Italy: Sign of the cross made in the air.

Latin America: Placing thumb and index together at tip as if snuffing a candle. Drawing the index, or index and middle fingers, representing a knife, quickly across the throat.

Netherlands: As hand, palm down, is drawn across the throat, it is swung inward, so that fingertips point toward throat.

Poland: Drawing finger across throat and pulling fist up behind his neck to indicate a noose.

: A Functional Approach to Gestures

Spain: One arm extended palm down and elbow bent in front of speaker; moving sharply from side to side. Drawing the finger across the throat, head inclined.

Spain, Latin America: Both arms extended, palms down, elbows bent in front of speaker, then arms drawn away from one another sharply, accompanying expressions of death, failure, ruin, or disappearance.

Syria: Drawing finger across throat.

DECEPTION

Europe, North America: Lowering of brows, gaze directly ahead, jaws tightly closed. Eyelids half-closed, look to side. Brows drawn together, forced smile.

Spain: Swinging the clenched hand forward, palm down and index extended, away from the chest in a half circle may accompany expressions suggesting "undetermining."

U.S.: Holding the right index and middle finger a little in front and to the right of the mouth, pointing to the left, moving the hand to the left, past the mouth and downward.

DECISION

Germany: Tightly closed mouth.

Kuwait, Iraq, Syria, Saudi Arabia: Shutting the eyes and holding out both hands with fingers pointed towards each other slowly so that fingertips touch. If successful, a trip may be taken; if not, it must be cancelled. Counting beads before taking a trip to decide whether or not to take a trip or embark upon some enterprise.

Spain: Verbal suggestion of clarity of thought can be accompanied by raising the fingertips of each hand, palms inward, to the forehead. Hands are withdrawn suddenly and held in front of speaker, palms inward.

U.S.: Protruding lower jaw.

DEFIANCE

England: Chin raised. Snapping fingers at adversaries.

France, Netherlands, U.S.: Tongue is stuck out in the direction of someone.

Italy: Clenched fist, thumb protruding between middle and ring finger toward the heavens.

Jordan, Lebanon: Left arm raised slowly, right hand passed beneath it simultaneously as body turns slightly.

Lebanon, Syria: Both fists clenched at waist level, thumbs extended in opposite directions.

Saudi Arabia: Right index hooked over the tip of the nose.

U.S.: Raising the fist with the middle finger extended.

DENIAL

Europe, North America: Index shaken from side to side, arm extended forward, palm outward.

France: Hand raised, palm forward, or sometimes simply the index extended, shakes rapidly sideways. Equivalent to shaking the head.

DEPART

Africa: Right arm extended forward, index of right hand moved back and forth. Right hand placed on shoulder of the person departing, left pointing in direction in which person is going.

Argentina, Uruguay: Hand is shaken energetically, as though shaking a thermometer, so that the fingers snap.

Colombia: Forearm horizontal to waist; fingers held together and extended, palm facing away from body; hand moves out sharply to side. Finger extended in direction of desired departure signifies a request to someone to depart. Kicking as if kicking a ball is a command to someone to leave. Palm facing body, hand moves back and forth.

Egypt: Fingers held in pear-shaped configuration so that they point forward, then opened quickly.

France: Edge of left hand is brought down smartly over the crook of the right elbow. Wagging hands to signify "Let's get out of here." Describing a sudden departure needs two hands: the left, fingers held straight, moves upwards from waist level to smack into the palm of the right hand moving downward; a restricted version of the popular and extremely vulgar bicep crunch.

France, Italy and Europe: Flat right hand, held with thumb uppermost, flicked slightly upward, while flat left hand, thumb uppermost, is chopped down on right wrist.

Israel: Hand held with palm downward, fingers flicking away from the body.

Italy: One hand horizontal at middle of body, palm up, the other hand rapidly moves over it from wrist to beyond fingertips, palm inward, signifies "Let's beat it." Edge of left hand makes chopping motion against the right wrist to represent "Go away."

Netherlands: Arm extended sideways, index extended. Right arm extended forward, palm flat, facing left; left arm bent, so that lower arm extends across chest, palm down; elbow of right arm placed on top of left wrist, making a downward chopping motion. Palm downward, hand flicking away from the body which indicates "Leave me in peace." Head inclined to one side and moved quickly to the other while looking angrily at someone indicates "Scram!"

Nigeria: Winking at children if the parents want them to leave the room.

Portugal: Rapid lifting of the head can be a command.

U.S.: Palm pushed vertically forward.

DESPAIR

Albania: Hands grasp beard. Hands grasp cheeks.

Europe, North America: Eyebrows drawn down, fixed look, facial muscles relaxed, head bowed low.

France: Rolling eyes and giving an expression of pain on the face. Elbows against body, hands clasped at the height of the shoulders; from a position touching the chest they are lowered.

Germany: Raising arms and letting them fall flat-handed downward.

Italy: Hands grasps throat, eyes closed

Netherlands: Eyes raised, hands, palms up, spread diagonally in front. Eyes closed, one hand covering eyes.

Russia: Hand makes motion of winding rope around neck, then it is raised above head, making a tugging motion. Flat hand, palm down, is drawn across neck below chin.

Switzerland: Wringing hands above one's head.

U.S.: Throwing up the hands in the air to represent despair.

DESPERATION

France: Elbows close to body, hands raised as high as the shoulders. Right hand hits left palm to palm. Hands remain united and together are raised to touch breast, then lowered. At same time head is shaken.

DETERMINATION

Africa: Right hand beats on breast.

England: Kicking oneself on the shins. Fists clenched. Gritting teeth.

DIRECTION

Africa: Open hand, palm down, moved up and down. Lips turned in the direction the gesturer wants to indicate.

England: Jerking head in the direction of sound and movement.

Europe, U.S.: Hand and arm extended, index pointing in specific direction.

France: Slowly closing one eye. Index pointed, the other fingers in any other position, usually turned back.

U.S.: Jerking thumb over shoulder indicates a backward direction. Left hand held out flat, palm down, right index runs across it, signifies "across." Pointing upward. Index swung forward and down in a curve to indicate "forward." Point up very high and look upward. Hold out flat left, palm down, and above it hold right in the same way (over or above). Index extended, pointing down. Pointing down, hand swung in small circle (here).

DISAPPOINTMENT

Africa: Fingers of both hands tense, pointing down, are agitated back and forth in a semi-circular fashion in front of body.

Colombia: Thumb rests between chin and lower lip while fingers, extended, move from side to side. Thumb at corner of mouth, fingers extended, palm facing away from the body.

Europe, North America: Raised and frowning brows, jaw lowered, corners of mouth drawn down. Biting lower lip.

Spain: Right hand makes rapid movement from right to left in front of mouth a if waving something off, or a fanlike folding inward of the fingers. Arms thrown back, corners of mouth pulled down, lips open as if to curse.

DISBELIEF

Africa: Fingers of right hand scratch top of head.

Arab: Hitting teeth with tongue, simultaneously lifting head quickly.

Argentina: Pulling an imaginary beard.

Argentina, Uruguay: Half-closed fist at chest height, curved index extended slightly forward, hand moves toward person addressed as though offering first joint of index finger. One or both hands, palm outward, raised and pulled back slowly until almost touching toward shoulders.

Colombia: Index moves lightly up an down throat several times. Often accompanied by widening of lips. Hand cupped, palm up, at neck approximately six inches below chin. Not usually used directly in front of speaker who is disbelieved. Lips tight, slowing widening, sometimes head nods, accompanied by uttering "m-hmmm."

Europe, North America: One corner of mouth drawn down, one cheek raised, partly closing one eye.

France: Fingers of right hand, loosely cupped, scrub right cheek upwards and downwards; corners of mouth dropping. Index pulls down lower eyelid. Right hand fingers tie, eye half closed, mouth puckered in condescending smile. Shoulders hunched, face shows pain, right hand jiggles vigorously at approximately chin level as if burned, air is sucked in suddenly or quick up and down whistling sound is made. Sometimes only index is jiggled.

Germany: Shaking head.

Jordan, Lebanon, Saudi Arabia: While someone is speaking, turn head or back to him indicating disbelief or unwillingness to listen further.

Latin America: Winking. Nose held with index and thumb, head ducked as if to say "I' m going under so that it passes me by."

Portugal: Slowing swinging head from side to side.

: A Functional Approach to Gestures

Turning head aside.

Saudi Arabia: Half-closed hand placed in front of abdomen, then turned slightly to indicate that the person addressed is a liar. Lightly hitting thumbnails of both hands together. Flip hands up and out in front of body and extend the tongue.

Moving tongue in and out of mouth rapidly.

Spain, Latin America: Raising arm vertically from neutral position nears side of head, then dropping it to original position.

U.S.: Motion of using a shovel to throw manure over one's shoulder; usually humorous. Head of gesticulator turned away from the speaker; one arm raised, palm facing speaker; often hand is lowered briskly. Exposing white of eye with finger. One eye sometimes half closed, fist clenched, thumb points to speaker. Eyes fixed and straight ahead, hands folded in front of mouth. Slowly raising and lowering one eyebrow. Eyebrows raising, corners of mouth drawn down. Index and little finger extended. Indexes of both hands extended and placed along temples, pointing upward. Pointing the indexes of both hands, placing them along the temples, pointing upward. Laying right index on right side of nose.

Venezuela: Hat worn askew.

DISCOURAGEMENT

Brazil: Extended index pointing down.

Europe, North America: Head drawn backwards, frown, eyes squinting, raised nose, corners of mouth drawn down. Eyebrows drawn down, fixed glance, facial muscles relaxed, head bowed, lips drawn down.

Italy: Fingers close together, palms pressed together, thumbs depressed, hands rhythmically moved up and down.

DISGUST

Africa: Lower lip is pushed forward, corners of mouth turned down.

Colombia: Hand, palm down, placed horizontally in front of chest. Hand, palm down, put on top of head.

England: Nose is held while an imaginary lavatory chain is pulled.

Europe: Lips turned outward and pulled apart, upper lip raised, mouth assumes rectangular form, nostrils flare, eyes closed.

Europe, North America: One hand upright near the face, palm out, or both hands extended forward.
Netherlands: Hand, palm down, at shoulder level, fingers apart and slightly bent, tongue extruded to express "Yuck!"

Spain, Latin America: Rubbing the hands together may

accompany verbal expression of repugnance.

U.S.: Thumb and index placed on slightly extruded tongue.

DISLIKE

Africa: Mouth closed, corners of mouth drawn down, forehead wrinkled.

Italy: Blowing whistle in the street; usually down in a protest group.

Russia: Flicking the ear while referring to someone.

U.S.: Wrinkling nose.

DISMAY

Europe: Sighing and shaking head.

Netherlands: Eyebrows raised, hand placed over mouth. Hand covers mouth.

DISPLEASURE

Brazil: Stamping on the floor in a theater.

Netherlands: Tapping thumbnails together as if applauding with the thumbnails is a form of ironical applause indicating displeasure.

DISSATISFACTION

Russia: Index extended and placed with the tip against the temple in imitation of the barrel of a gun; jocular or ironic dissatisfaction with oneself or someone else.

Saudi Arabia, Syria: Exhale very slowly.

U.S.: Holding nose with thumb and index. Grunting.

DISTRESS

Netherlands: Flat hand strikes top of head.

U.S.: Grimace while shaking right hand.

DOUBT

Brazil: Flat hand taps both cheeks, one after the other. Clicking the tongue.

Latin America: Moving the open extended hand, palm out, back and forth several times and with a wrist movement describing a semi-circle.

U.S.: Rolling the eyes. Raising the eyebrows.

DRINK

Africa: Right hand raises an imagined glass to the open mouth. Right hand, placed to mouth, imitates the action of emptying a glass. Hands, side to side and palms up, indicate throwing of water to the mouth, or a receptacle for water to drink. Fingertips of right hand, palm inward, scratching the Adam's apple.

Arab: Index and little finger extended from closed hand and brought to mouth while head is tilted back a little.

Colombia: Space between extended index and thumb indicates size of drink desired. Thumb extended, pointing to mouth, little finger raised; hand rocks back and forth.

Europe: Thumb raised repeatedly to the mouth.

France: Closed fist, thumb extended and moved toward mouth until tip of thumb touches lips. Touching lips with the tip of the extended thumb, other fingers closed.

Germany: Putting cupped hand to the mouth.

Italy: A thumb jabbed at the mouth. Thumb extended, fist clenched and moved toward mouth.

Latin America: Extended thumb with other fingers clenched directed towards a glass or cup may mean to pour. Fist clenched and thumb pointing towards the mouth. Fingers either held tightly clenched or extended at right angles to the thumb. Can also indicate drunkenness. Right thumb and small finger extended, other fingers folded into palm, the hand is moved toward the mouth several times.

Mexico: Hand raised in front of body, thumb and little finger extended, knuckles outward to indicate "Would you like a drink?"

Poland: Flicking a finger against the neck invites a close friend to join the gesturer in a drink.

Russia: Hand held in front of stomach, index and middle finger extended to the side: invitation to share the cost of a bottle of vodka. Hand raised toward mouth, thumb and little finger extended to signify "Let's down a few."

Saudi Arabia: Holding thumb side of right fist on mouth.

Spain: Right hand closed, thumb raised and moved to the mouth in the manner of a spigot.

Ukraine: Hand raised to the level of the eyes, index and thumb extended about one inch apart.

U.S.: Making a "C" or a "T" with the index or indexes signifies a request for coffee or tea. Tongue protrudes over lower lip; often comic.

EATING

Africa: Tips of index and thumb of right hand joined and alternately moved toward and away from the mouth. Right hand closed, imitates pulling an object from the mouth to the right.

Argentina: Open hand, palm down, strikes sideways against gesticulator's waist.

Colombia, U.S.: Open hand rubbed back and forth across abdomen. Cupped fingers of one hand move back and forth in front of open mouth.

France: Hand moved to mouth, all fingers united at tips. Mouth wide open, fingers of one hand bunched at tips and brought to the mouth. Chin raised, fingers and thumb of the right hand pinched together, curved and jerked two or three times toward the open mouth; eyebrows raised.

Italy: Tips of thumb and index applied around the mouth with rapid alternations in a vertical and horizontal direction. Beating the ribs with the flat of the hand. Hand lifted to mouth, imaginary food trickled in as in eating spaghetti by hand. Uniting tips of all fingers of one hand, move them repeatedly to the mouth and away again.

Netherlands: Open hand moved in circular fashion over abdomen, accompanied by dissatisfied expression that gesturer is hungry. Mouth open, pointing into it. Closed hand, thumb sticking up; move from wrist toward mouth.

Spain, Latin America: Fingers of right hand curved, tips joined and repeatedly moved to the mouth.

EMBARRASSMENT

Argentina, Uruguay: Biting the lower lip in regret for saying something one should not have said.

England: Dropping the eyes.

Germany: Blushing and casting eyes down.

Spain, Latin America: Hand raised to mouth, covering mouth with fingers.

U.S.: Shuffling the feet. Shifting from one foot to another. Placing fingers of one hand over the mouth. Blushing.

EMPHASIS

Colombia: Fingers of each hand joined at tips, tap chest. Fingers extended, heel of palm strikes forehead. Hand sweeps upward and outward, palm facing away from the body. Fist strikes palm or a surface such as a table once or several times.

England: Leaning forward and jabbing with index finger to show emphasis. Laying a hand on listener's sleeve.

Europe, North America: Open hand in front, palm turned out, hand raised, fingertips up.

France: Thumb in contact with tip of middle or index finger, forming a ring.

Italy: Both hands are held in front of the chest, all fingertips touching and shaken up and down. The 'hand purse' : tips of fingers brought together as if holding a small object, palm upward. As a baton-gesture, i.e. accompanying speech rhythmically, the gesture is usually made when the speaker is making a fine point or requiring more precision; as such it is very common. But the gesture can also be performed independently of speech and it can signify a request for clarity.

Portugal: Winking an eye to hint at emphasis.

Spain, Latin America: Lowering joined thumb and index of one hand, palm down, directly in front of gesticulator's face to a position in which fingers are spread apart widely. Executed sharply, ending at waist level. Suggest ultimatum. Bunched fingers of one hand pushed toward imaginary point in the air. Raising the slightly clenched fingers of one hand, palm up, to or above the speaker's chest. Occasionally both hands. When performed with one hand, the fingers may be rotated back and forth with the wrist serving as an axis. Accompanies expressions indicating a nucleus of an entity or survey or synopsis.

U.S.: Hand raised, index and middle fingers extended, forming a "V." Inserting hand or finger into clenched fingers of other hand.

ENCOURAGEMENT

Africa: Both hands hold upper arms of someone standing in front of gesturer and shake him.

Colombia: Clapping someone on the shoulder or patting him on the back of the hand.

England: Squeezing and patting the arm. Spitting on fingertips or palms and rubbing hands together.

India: Thumb extended and turned up signifies

encouraging verification.

Spain: Raising both spread hands, palms up, as if actually raising an object with the open hands.

U.S.: Forearm level, thrust forward, hand brought back toward body. Hand pats another football player's buttocks once. Stroking hand of listener in silence.

ENTHUSIASM

Africa: Arms raised above head, head agitated.

Brazil: Wiggling lobe of ear with thumb and index of right hand. Extreme: right hand is passed behind head and lobe of left ear is wiggled.

Colombia: Hands clasped in front of chest, usually female. Hands raised, fingers extended, mouth often open.

Mexico: Vigorous vertical movement of forearm, snapping of middle finger against ball of thumb.

EVASIVENESS

England, U.S.: Avoiding eye contact.

U.S.: Shifting attention and fidgeting.

EXCITEMENT

Africa: Air released through lips so as to produce a whistle.

: A Functional Approach to Gestures

Colombia: Hands in front of body, palms facing about twelve inches apart, hands are then clasped. Open hand covers mouth. Often in context of impending danger.

Universal: Biting lips.

EYE CONTACT

Arab: Long, direct eye contact is important among Arab men.

Finland, Netherlands, Argentina, Australia: Eye contact is important.

Ghana: Children are trained not to maintain eye contact with adults, since it is regarded as disrespectful.

Japan, Korea, Thailand, Zimbabwe: Impolite to maintain prolonged eye contact.

Norway, Sweden: Eye contact is important in toasting, both in raising and in lowering the glass.

Saudi Arabia: Strong eye contact is favored.

FAILURE

Africa: A reaction to failure is the covering of the mouth with the right hand.

Argentina: Fingertips of one hand joined and pointed upwards, then suddenly released and spread in shape of tulip blossom.

FAMILIARITY

Middle East: Lighting another person's cigarette, especially of the hand holding the light is steadied by that of the other person.

U.S.: Not touching another person of higher status.

FAREWELL

Africa: Male friends in parting oftenpress the middle finger of one hand participating in the handshake against that of the other participating hand, and as the grip is released, snap it against the base of the thumb.

Colombia: Men rise when man or woman leaves room. Women may or may not rise. The more formal the occasion, the more likely everyone is to rise. Fingertips to lips, then thrown forward; considered intimate and casual. Hand moves more slowly, fingers closed together than in the U.S. goodbye wave. Fingers spread apart, sometimes whole arm waves vigorously. Hand placed to temple in military salute.

Denmark: Departing person after divorce takes a piece of a linen cloth, of which the remaining person takes the other piece.

England, Scandinavia, Netherlands, Germany, Austria, Belgium, Portugal, Malta, Tunisia, Greece, Turkey: Palm-out wave is common.

France: Arm extended in the direction of someone, hand relaxed but agitated in a lively manner up and

: A Functional Approach to Gestures

down, palm facing down; familiar.

India, Mongolia: Salutation by nose contact.

Italy: Arm bent, hand approximately shoulder level, fingers cupped, hand and arm moved repeatedly and slightly up and down. Hand waving, palm toward face of gesticulator at arm's length. Palm upward and fingers alternately clenched and outstretched.

Italy, Sicily, Sardinia: The palm-in wave is common.

Jordan, Lebanon, Saudi Arabia, Syria: Holding up right hand with palm facing backward and moving fingers and hand back.

Russia: All ages may suggest immediately before the departure of a friend that they sit together in silence for a few minutes. It is customary, at least for the departing friend, to sit on the suitcases.

Spain: Arm raised, all fingers except thumb flapped, palm facing gesticulator. Hand extended short distance, palm faces gesticulator, tips of fingers repeatedly lowered and raised rapidly, often tapping base of palm.

U.S.: Waving hand up and down. Flat hand held high, palm down and forward, fingers quickly waved up and down. Hand moves up and down at approximately face level, palm down.

FATIGUE

Africa: Curved index of right hand drawn across forehead as if to wipe off perspiration, then flicked outward to throw it off. Right hand at waist, head inclined forward.

Colombia: Hands palm to palm, placed along cheek, head inclined to side, resting on back of hand. Eyes often closed simultaneously. Hand, palm to face, moves slowly across brow or eyes. Fingers extended, tapping open mouth lightly and repeatedly; impolite in formal social context.

France: Eyes closed, head inclined laterally, cheek reposes on back of one hand, which is joined to the other palm to palm.

Spain: Putting head sideways with eyes closed, resting it upon the right hand.

U.S.: Fist placed in each eye. Supporting face with hands. Dragging the feet. Yawning.

FEAR

Arab: Grasping one's beard.

Argentina, Uruguay: Fingertips of one or both joined and pointed upwards, hands move back and forth while the fingers open and close.

England: Clutching arms and hunching shoulders.

Europe: Shuddering. Shaking of the body

Europe, North America: Hands upright near the face, palms out.

France: Hand purse, i.e., fingers joined at the tips, palm upward.

Germany: Forehead furrowed in pain, eyes opened wide.

Italy: Hands beaten together.

Netherlands: Flat hand slightly extended in front, edge down, makes chopping motion.

Universal: Deeply arched brows. The eyebrow flash is part of a facial recoiling.

U.S.: Stepping back. Holding up both hands, palm forward.

FINISHED

Africa: Elbows spread to the sides and vigorously brought back to the sides. Open hands, palm outwards, crossed in front of chest, then spread apart, moving left and right respectively. Palm of right hand slaps palm of left hand.

Colombia: Arms crossed in front of body, palms down; then arms move out to the sides, palms still down.

France: Pulling a finger across the throat to indicate bankruptcy. Turn up hand, palm up.

Italy: Extended index raised once or twice

Netherlands: One hand moves upward, the other downward, palms facing each other.

Portugal: Point of thumb placed under chin, hand quickly moves forward.

Russia: The edge of the flat right hand, palm down,

strikes the back of one's neck, or, with the edge of thumb-side, the front of the neck at the side of the Adam's apple.

Saudi Arabia: Palms placed together so that fingers are pointing forward, then twist hands in opposite directions but keep them in contact.

Spain: Cutting across the body with the open hand, fingers extended and palm inward from shoulder of one side to waist of the other.

U.S.: Crossing arms at waist level and extending them in an arc, fingers extended, palms down, specifically used by referee at prize fights.

Yemen: Hitting side of one's neck with right hand.

FLATTERY

Argentina, Uruguay: Pulling an earlobe with two fingers signifies that the person indicated is in agreement.

Germany: Turning of the thumb.

South Korea: Palms together horizontally at waist level and then twist back and forth to indicate excessive compliments, i.e. "lip service."

U.S.: Hand twists tip of nose.

FLIRTING

Colombia: Winking with eye.

Europe, North America: Head leaning to side, eyebrows

raised, lips smiling and slightly pursed.

Lebanon: Men make chirping sound in flirting with woman.

Lebanon, Saudi Arabia: Eyebrows moving up and down rapidly.

Russia: Narrowing the eyes denotes apprehension or the challenging invitation to flirtation in women.

Syria: Thumb placed in mouth sideways and bitten, then removed and shaken.

U.S.: Rolling eyes. The "eyebrow flash" perhaps popularized by Groucho Marx, usually combined with a smile. The flirting female at first smiles at her partner and lifts her eyebrows with a quick, jerky movement upward so that the eye slit is briefly enlarged. Flirting men show the same movement. After this most initial, obvious turning-toward the person in the flirt situation, then turns away. The raised eyebrow breaks the taboo of the sustained eye contact and is used in everyday flirting to signal interest in a person and is also used as a tactic in prostitution. If a woman returns a stare and her eyebrows are raised, it means she is interested. Women will tilt head to the side and expose her neck.

FOOLISHNESS

Arab: Right index makes circular motion near right temple, head tilted slightly. Right index taps right temple, then is thrown out to side of head as head is

tilted slightly to one side and brows are wrinkled.
Africa: Index pointed at temple.

Colombia: Index points to temple and makes circular motion. Index taps temple.

France: Placing the index at the temple, making the movement of drilling it into the head. Tapping one's forehead with the index slightly curved.

Germany: Mouth open.

Italy: Fingertips of one hand are held together at the elbow of the other arm, fingertips of other hand are also held together while hand is waved back and forth. Tapping the center of the forehead. Thumb against temple, hand open.

Latin America: Raising index and middle finger to forehead. Extending lower lip, or pulling the lower lip downward with the index. Raising and lowering the cupped hand as if trying the weight of an object.

Netherlands: Relentless tapping of forehead with tip of index.

Portugal: Finger pointing at forehead.

Russia: Hands, open palms forward, flapped from temples to earlobes. Tip of thumb pressed to right temple, palm open, facing forward and pivoting up and down on the thumb.

Spain, Latin America: Raising index of one hand to temple and twisting it back and forth slowly or simply raising index to temple.

FRIENDSHIP

Africa: Index of left hand curls around extended little finger of right hand.

China: One's right hand shakes one's left hand while one looks in the direction of the other person.

England: Linking little fingers of right hands, shaking them up and down.

Europe, North America: Both arms extended full length at level of shoulders, hands open, palms facing each other.

Lebanon: Indexes of right hands joined.

Lebanon, Syria, Jordan, Saudi Arabia: Patting another person's shoulder with right hand.

Middle East, Korea, China, Vietnam: Holding hands among men while walking is a sign of friendship and mutual respect.

Morocco: Two indexes extended and placed parallel with each other.

Polynesia: Holding up branches of trees, canoe paddles, stick, poles decorated with feathers, white flags, pieces of cloth in token of friendship.

Saudi Arabia: Index and middle finger together, other fingers pressed tightly into palm under the thumb. Touching tip of nose with back of right hand, simultaneously moving head back and forth as nose is touched.

U.S.: Holding up two fingers close together. Middle finger crosses index of same hand.

FRUSTRATION

Colombia: Fist bangs slowly and repeatedly on table; lips usually tight.

Europe, Brazil: Index passed under someone else's nose indicates an unexpected failure.

France: Elbows against body, hands at shoulder height, right palm clasps left, both hands remain joined. From a position touching the chest they are lowered. Striking forehead with a flat hand. Shoulders raised and lowered rapidly once or twice. Often reinforced by sigh, eyes directed upward.

Russia: Flat hand, thumb extended outward, strikes forehead, then turned downward so that fingertips are at the brow line, pointing diagonally down; usually referring to oneself. Right fist raised to side of head and held there for a moment; can refer to oneself or someone else.

Spain, Latin America: Open hand, fingers slightly bent, pressed against abdomen. Shoulders shrugged, both arms raised sharply, palms facing upward and fingers spread.

GOSSIP

Africa: Lips pressed together between teeth. Protruded tongue moves rapidly from left to right.

Italy: Thumb and middle finger opening and closing while moving the hand away from the body as if cutting with scissors.

Russia: Hand, palm forward, placed behind an ear, signifies that the person referred to is a gossip.

Spain: Index touches tip of tongue.

GRATITUDE

Greece: Left hand laid upon chest.

Lebanon, Saudi Arabia, Syria: Kissing the back of the right hand, then raising it, palm up.

Mexico: Hand open and raised, then given a 90 degree turn.

Netherlands: Bowing as expression of gratitude for applause. Tip of extended index placed at the bill of an imaginary cap, then moved quickly upward and outward.

Saudi Arabia: Palm of right hand placed on chest, head bowed, eyes closed. After a man dances he kneels before the musician who wipes the dancer's cheeks with his head-cloth to show an expression of gratitude.

GREETING

Africa: Arms raised over the level of the head, hands open, palms toward the front. Forehead touching the ground in greeting a high ranking person. Holding each other by the hand, two men bump chest against chest. Young women greet each other by bumping their buttocks against each other. Holding each other's hands, women greet by putting cheek against cheek. Son greets father with handshake, but does not look into his eyes. Instead, he looks slightly to the left.

Arab: Right hand reaches down as if to take dust from the ground, then is raised to chest, mouth, and forehead.

Brazil: Hands clasped above head and shaken slightly; common among athletes.

Colombia: Male grasps forearm or upper arm of another male, who grasps upper arm or shoulder of the former, sometimes with patting motion. Women usually grasp one another's forearms; more common among urban women. Bow of head or upper part of body, standing or walking, is of minimum courtesy. Eyebrows raised and lowered quickly, often with nod or smile. Hand moving sharply from temple to side and up; informal.

Europe, North America: Head inclined forward, eyelids droop. Hand upright, palm inside, held at level of face, arm half bent, moving of the tips of the fingers from forehead outward.

Fiji: Nodding and then flicking the eyebrows upward.

Fiji, Malaya: Sniffing without joining noses as a salute.

Germany: Kiss either on cheeks or lips, together with embrace. Rapping the edge of a table with the knuckles is the customary greeting and farewell of German university students for their professors.

: A Functional Approach to Gestures

Guam: Raising eyebrows. Chin slightly lifted.

India: Person of low social position falls flat on the ground with hands folded in front. Pulling one another's ears in salutation. Bowing, touching feet and raisng hand to head.

Italy: Hand held at shoulder height, palm up, fingers waggled inward as if scratching is common.

Japan: Bowing used as a sign of respect and humility. Lower ranking person bows first and deeper to higher ranking person.

Jordan, Saudi Arabia: Tips of fingers of right hand touched to forehead, then chest and back to forehead while bowing slightly.

Latin America: One or two hearty slaps on back of other person.

Lebanon, Jordan, Syria, Saudi Arabia: Right hand pressed against chest. When two men meet, they kiss each other on the cheeks, first one cheek, then the other, while placing hands on each other's shoulders.

Malaysia: Bows deeply to knee level, placing the right hand on the ground; repeated three times before approaching person of superior status. Once in front, places head between the person's hands, symbolically offering it to them.

Netherlands: Arm raised, open hand waved backward and forward. Closed fist, lower arm raised, i.e. Communist salute.

New Guinea: Squeezing nostrils with index and thumb of left hand, and pointing to navel with index of right hand; friendly greeting.

North America: Hand raised to head-level or above and waggled back and forth, left to right, is common for hello or good-bye. Eskimos greet each other by banging the other party with a hand either on the head or shoulders. Rubbing noses as sign of affection and greeting.

Phillipines: Bending very low, raising one foot in the air with the knee bent.

Polynesia: Men welcome each other by embracing and rubbing each other's back. Rubbing noses as sign of affection and greeting. Sticking out the tongue.

Portugal: Bowing in gratitude shows greater intensity of emotions than inclining the head.

Russia: Handshake often followed by powerful embrace. After a long absence, men customarily greet each other with the triple kiss: the welcoming male embraces his friend, while the latter kisses him three times, starting at the right. Men bow to each other combined with a powerful handshake.

Saudi Arabia: When two men meet, they embrace and kiss. Man kisses woman on forehead; son kisses mother on lips or forehead; girls kiss older woman on forehead.

U.S.: Raising the hand with the palm outward and the arm bent at the elbow. Hand occasionally waved from right to left, but fingers not waved. Forearm waved if the person is close by; the whole arm if at a distance. Slapping the back of a person. Good friends may pass close to each other and wink as greeting. Forefinger pointed, thumb raised, then brought down in imitation of the hammer of a pistol. A wink often accompanies this gesture. Waving the hand back and forth in greeting.

HANDSHAKE

Africa: Handshake is common and often accompanied by cracking or snapping of the fingers.

Bolivia: Whenever two friends meet and chat, their greeting usually includes a handshake and a hearty clap on the back.

China: Clapping one's hand as in applause.

Colombia: Frequently used and omission may be a discourtesy.

Egypt: At pre-wedding ceremony, the bride's proxy and the bridegroom join hands; the parties sit on the ground face to face, grasping one another's right hands, raising the thumbs and pressing them one against the other.

Europe, North America: Limp handshake is regarded as unpleasant, indicating weakness and effeminacy.

Finland: No bodily contact other than a handshake.

France: Handshake performed by one person, his right hand shaking his left while he is looking at someone who is generally at too great a distance for the former to shake hands with him; informal. Hand raised above level of the head, turned toward someone, fingers extended and slightly separated, hand agitated slightly in the direction from thumb to little finger, palm inward; friendly, informal.

India, Thailand, Cambodia: Hands palm to palm vertically in front of chest, accompanied by slight bow. Pulling one another's ears in salutation.

Japan, North and South Korea: If western style handshake is used, simultaneous eye contact is avoided as disrespectful.

Kenya: Friends shake hands with light slap palm against palm, followed by a mutual grasp of cupped fingers.

Mexico: Friends greet with conventional handshake followed by grasping each other's thumb.

Middle East: A gentle grip is appropriate; a firm grip suggest aggressiveness.

Middle East, Europe: Firm grip used in American-style handshake can signal aggressiveness, especially if it is accompanied by more arm pumps than are considered normal in the host country.

Russia: Male friends may start the greeting with a firm handshake and continue with a "bear hug." Clapping of the hands.

South Africa: Sprinkling sand or mud over one's body.

Spain: Handshake rare as a greeting in face-to-face communities.

Taiwan, Hong Kong, Singapore, China: Conventional handshake is customary greeting, sometimes accompanied by a slight bob of the head.

U.S.: Strong, firm handshake without excessive pumping is the norm among both men and women.

HELPLESSNESS

Argentina: While exhibiting a pitiful expression, the person closes their eyes and wrings their hands.

England: Spreading the hands and shrugging.

France: Lifting up the shoulders and holding up hands at height of the head.

Germany: Turning up the palms.

Italy: Shoulders lifted, one hand extended, palm up.

HUMILITY

Arab: In greeting one bows the head and lays the hand upon the chest as a sign of humility and gratitude.

Asia: Arms crossed on the chest so that the hands lie on the shoulders while executing a deep bow.

Europe: Head bowed, eyes raised, mouth smiling, cheeks raised.

HUNGER

Africa: Right hand repeatedly slaps stomach, or both hands rub up and down on stomach.

Colombia: Both fists held against abdomen, mouth open.

France: Hand is moved to the mouth, fingers joined; considered vulgar.

Italy: The right hand is outstretched, plam down, and the hand is moved back and forth horizontally at waist level.

Jordan, Lebanon, Libya, Syria, Saudi Arabia: Right palm pressed on abdomen and moved in circle.

HURRY UP

Argentina, Uruguay: Open palm at level of stomach or chest rises very rapidly.

France: Palm of one hand give sharp blow to palm of the other, which simultaneously rises as if to catapult an object resting on it into the air. Flat of hand is swung backward and forward repeatedly.

Russia: Snapping fourth finger and thumb as a signal to hasten a response.

Saudi Arabia: Tip of right index placed on tongue, then on tip of nose.

U.S.: Drawing in flat hand, palm toward gesturer, vigorously and repeatedly several times.

IGNORANCE

Arab: Shrugging the shoulders, hands extended, palms up, head tilted slightly to one side.

Argentina: Fingernails of the closed fingers one hand rub the heel of the hand as they move rapidly and energetically outward.

Colombia: Hand, palms facing out, held up in front of body, then moved slightly to sides. Slight pursing of lips usually accompanies gesture. One hand raised in front or to side of body, palm out; often mouth tightened, head tilted. Scratching head.

Europe, India: Jerking the fingers.

Europe, North America: Palms facing upward, arms bent at elbows, shoulders shrugged; indicates a refusal to accept responsibility. Shoulders hunched, eyebrows raised, corners of mouth drawn down.

France: Shoulders raised, elbows close to body, hands raised a little to both sides, palms turned up and facing forward from a position slightly in the rear of the body.

Portugal: The "chin flick": fingernails of one hand brush forward under the chin, then fingers flick outward.

U.S.: Raising high the eyebrows. Shrugging the shoulders, shaking head, raising right hand, palm up to level of shoulders, inclining head to one side.

IMPATIENCE

Africa: Fingers of one hand raised in succession, starting with the thumb, as if counting to five, five being the limit one can bear with patience. Open hands shaken in front of check or above the head, while feet stamp on the ground.

Argentina, Uruguay: Arm raised to head height, closed fist moves downward pulling an imaginary chain.

Brazil: Blowing on one's fingers.

Colombia: One hand slaps lightly against thigh and remains there for a momen. Often indicates imminent reprimand for a child.

France: Snapping thumb against middle or ring finger.

Netherlands: Flat hand, palm down, placed against or under chin. Fingers of one hand drum on a knee.

North America: Impatient audience slowly claps hands in rhythm.

Spain: Raising hand to a position over the head, or bringing it to rest on the back of the head.

U.S.: Fingers drumming on an object. Tapping foot several times on ground. Arms may be akimbo or folded across chest.

INDIFFERENCE

Argentina, Uruguay: Lower lip thrust forward over upper lip.

Brazil: Clicking the tongue.

Colombia: Head moved slowly from side to side.

France: Fingers of one hand close together, palm toward gesticulator, fingertips under chin, then had is suddenly flipped outward. Originated with flipping beard.

Italy: Tips of fingers rub slowly under the chin. Tips of fingers of one hand (except thumb) touch under the chin and then are flipped forward. Hand, palm inwards, fingers slightly bent, nails touching underside of chin is quickly whipped out to the front, indicating "What do I care?"

Spain: Can be exaggerated by arching the arms high above the shoulders with palms down. Middle finger snapped against thumb. Twisting open hand back and forth, thumb and fingers spread apart and palm facing away from speaker.

Spain, Latin America: Shrugging shoulders, head tilted, arms raised to side of body with elbows close to the body and palms facing up.

Spain, Portugal: Lower lips move forward, expulsion of air results in noise made with upper lip.

U.S.: Shrugging shoulders and shaking head.

INNOCENCE

Argentina, Uruguay: Arms raised straight above shoulder height, hands open, as if being search. Right hand clasps wrist of left hand behind back, as though in handcuffs.

France: Hands flat, palms outward and separated.

Spain: Accompanying disclaimer of blame, arms are raised to the side of the speaker, palms up.

INTELLECTUAL

Africa: Hand gently caresses forehead.

Colombia: Index taps lightly against temple or forehead or is simply placed against temple.

Italy: Placing forefinger to the forehead

Netherlands: Index tapping the temple. Tip of index placed against temple.

Spain, Latin America: Hand, fingers extended, palm facing speaker, is brought to the side of the head and the rigid fingers are pushed back and forth.

INTERROGATION

Africa: Chin raised in direction of someone and remaining raised.

Colombia: Hand extended in front, palm up, chin and eyebrows may be raised.

England: Brows raised to signal inquiry.

Europe, India: Backward nod of the head.

France: Hand extended slightly, palm up, shrugging shoulders.

Italy: Both hands held half cupped, palm up, fingertips pointing toward speaker, thumb pressed against index. Fingertips of each hand are united, pointing up, both hands held in front of body, palms turned in, hands moved slightly up and down.

Netherlands: In a hopeless situation, the gesture signals "What do we do now?" Eyebrows raised, head jerked backwards signals a silent inquiry.

Saudi Arabia: Earlobe rubbed with tips of right forefinger and thumb.

Spain, Latin America: Arms raised.

U.S.: Look, nod, brows raised.

INVITATION

Lebanon: Rubbing the back of one's neck with palm of right hand indicating that the gesturer would like to meet the woman to whom the gesture is made.

Netherlands: Arms extended slightly forward, towards a buffet.

Spain, Portugal, Morocco: Right hand extended, palm down, fingers pointing down.

U.S.: Pointing at another person may signify an invitation to join in going somewhere.

JOY

Bolivia: Slapping back of head in anger and in joy.

Brazil: Cracking one's knuckles.

Europe, North America: Biting of lower lip, raising eyebrows, lips and check extended. Lips extended in grin pushing up cheeks to form wrinkles under eyesd, brows raised, forming lines across forehead.

France: Clapping of hands.

Germany: Rubbing of hands. Weeping

Japan: In general, the Japanese smile when they are sad, happy, apologetic, angry, or confused. They do not smile for official photographs. Smiling is usually equated with frivolous or irresponsible behavior.

Korea: Bride never smiles for photographs as it is believed to bring bad luck. Smiling or laughter is sometimes an expression of embarrassment. Koreans do not smile for official photographs.

Lebanon, Jordan, Syria, Saudi Arabia: Hitting right thigh with palm of right hand.

U.S.: Arms extended over head and slightly to the side, hands clenched, head thrown back, face upwards.

JUDGMENT

Argentina, Uruguay: Flat hand strikes thumb and index of closed fist.

Italy: Both arms extended forward horizontally, both hands in same position. Tips of index and thumb turned down and forming a cone, as an imitation of a scale.

Saudi Arabia: Judge ties person's hands together with a head-cloth which indicates a person is a felon.

KILL

India, Sicily: Right hand closed, thumb out, pressed closed as in grasping knife, jerked thumb edge down.

Netherlands: Both closed hands held at waist level, palm down, thumbs extended and pointing horizontally toward each other as their tips are repeatedly brought together. Hand flat, edge down, makes chopping motion.

Spain: Pointing with one finger and drawing the other across the throat.

KISSING (used as a GREETING)

Asia: Kissing is considered an intimate sexual act and not permissible.

Bahrain, Saudi Arabia: Parent of a recently deceased son or daughter may kiss only on the shoulders in greeting.

Belgium, Russia: Three kisses are common; alternating sides, beginning on the left.

France: Both cheeks are kissed.

Latin America: Only one cheek is kissed.

Lebanon, Saudi Arabia, Syria: Two men kiss quickly on the lips in greeting.

New Zealand: Nose-pressing as kiss of welcome, of mourning and sympathy.

Russia: The lips touch the cheek.

Saudi Arabia: Woman kissing a man on the cheek in public without being married to him is punishable. Two men touch noses three times, then smack lips in greeting.

Spain: Used by Spanish women of all ages. One of the two women permits herself, by design or by accident, to be kissed by the other woman. The gesture often consists simply of brushing the other woman's cheek, almost always both, with the lips.

LAZINESS

Brazil: Hand supports chin accompanied by a vacant stare.

Mexico: Palm of one hand up as though to catch a drop of water, fingers bent, hand moving slightly up and down as though weighing something.

LUCK

Brazil: Index, middle, and ring finger extended touch the ground.

Colombia: On seeing three priests or three blacks, a girl will scratch her knee which will bring her luck in finding a husband soon.

England: Tossing a kiss or lifting one's hat to a chimney sweep, or having the
bride kissed by a sweep at the wedding means good luck.

: A Functional Approach to Gestures

Germany: Thumb of one or both hands tucked into the fist.

Italy: Index and little finger extended, pointing down, arm vertical.

Netherlands: Hands clasped, raised to level of face and shaken. Knocking knuckles on piece of wood indicates that someone has had good luck or that he hopes good luck will continue.

Paraguay: Crossed fingers can be considered offensive.

Saudi Arabia: Placing index sideways in mouth and biting it, then removing it, shaking it vigorously; reference to luck of another person.

Spain, Latin America: Knocking on wood.

U.S.: Thumb of one or both hands extended upwards fro fists. Index and middle
finger of one hand crossed. Middle finger of one or both hands crossed over
index. Knocking on wood.

MAGNITUDE

Africa: Thickness indicated by the right hand grasping the middle of the left forearm, or both hands grasping a knee, or the right hand grasping the left upper arm, or the index and thumb of one hand measuring the width of the thumb of the other, or both hands grasping the thigh, or both hands placed on the wrist. Right hand grasps left forearm. Index and thumb of right hand measure the thickness of the little finger of

Body Language

the left hand. Open hands, palms inward, moved up and down in front of the body. Open hands at level of head, palms facing one another across width of head and moved backward and forward. Hands joined in front of chest, then swung down and toward back, then right hand grasps left forearm.

One flat hand raised to height of head; gesture of women returning from fishing, indicating a large catch. Open right hand, palm down, held out at height of person, object, or plant. Open right hand, edge down, held out at height of a quadruped or flat object. Open right hand held vertically, fingertips pointing upward, at height of persons, shrubs, plants.

Argentina, Uruguay: Fingertips of one hand joined and pointing up, accompanied by upward glance; can be reinforced by a back and forth movement of wrist. Open palm at level of stomach or chest rises rapidly to indicate abundance.

Arab: Hitting or patting of the flat hand against the pocket, simultaneously looking alternatively at the person one is talking to and at one's pocket.

Brazil: Index extended parallel to thumb, the distance between them indicating the size of the drink.

Colombia: Index extended, thumb rests against first joint of index. To indicate the height of a child, the fingers held one above the other so that little finger is nearest to the ground. Improper to indicate the height of a child by holding hand so palm is turned to ground as this is used for animals and objects. Hand, fingers extended, held at certain height with edge of hand down to indicate the height of a human being. Flat palm of each hand, held vertically to indicate the length of an object.

Europe: Lips pursed, as in speaking of something small. Mouth is open wide in relating something large or important.

Europe, North America: Index of one hand points at tip of index of the other. Hands horizontally extended and apart, arms straight, palms down to indicate wide expanse.

France: Tips of thumb and index joined, forming a circle.

Italy: Thumb and index of one hand holding index of other hand to indicate small measurement.

Lebanon, Syria: Index extended from fist, tip of thumb placed on lower joint.

Mexico: Hand extended, palm down to indicate the height of objects.

Mexico, Guatemala: Palm turned down, indicating height of an animal; palm vertical and thumb thrust up, indicating height of child.

Netherlands: Hands, palms held flat and facing down, one some distance above the other. Right elbow placed in palm of left hand, right arm vertical, right hand at 90 degree angle to arm and turned inward. Hands held some distance one above other, palm of upper hand facing down and held flat, palm of lower hand facing up and held flat to indicate the height of an object. Hand held at some distance laterally from each other, palms flat and facing each other to indicate length of some object.

Saudi Arabia: Child raises both hands, palms forward, fingers spread

Spain: Smallness is indicated by joining tips of index and thumb. Palm facing either up or down. Or palm up, thumb on first joint of the index of same hand. Or snapping fingernails of index and thumb of same hand. With expressions suggesting a limited scope or range, small circles are described in the air with the spread fingers of one hand, palm down, at level of waist. Both hands raised to level of check, fingers extended, palms facing one another simultaneously.

Spain, Latin America: Lowering slightly bent arm in front of gesticulator, palm down to indicate shortness. Hand raised, palm down to level referred to verbally to indicate tallness. Raising bunched fingers of one hand to the level of the chest with palm facing speaker indicates " nothing." Expressions suggesting emergence or growth can be accompanied by raising bunched fingers of one hand, fingers upward, from the waist to approximately the level of the chest. Hands, palms down, fingers extended pushed away from each other at level of of gesticulator's waist. Gesture may accompany verbal behavior on topic of mass thought or activity.

U.S.: Cheeks filled with air as hands indicate girth of a fat person. Hand, fingers extended, held at certain height with palm down to indicate height of human being or animal.

: **A Functional Approach to Gestures**

MOCKERY

Africa: Both hands, open, forming contours of large stomach in front of abdomen. Open hands describe spheres on chest to indicate large breasts. Open hands pressed against chest to indicate flat breasts. Cheeks puffed out, hands raised and at some distance from each other on each side of the face indicating "You are this fat!" Cheeks puffed out in imitation of a case of mumps, open hands laid on cheeks. Tips of thumb, index, and middle finger joined and placed under the chin, indicating a sorcerer. Right hand grasps chin, mouth drawn in malicious smile. Hands, palms open and forwards, are placed behind ears, appearing to elongate them or each hand pulls each ear upwards. Also, hands placed to ears like wings. Flat hands, palms against cheeks, so that the hands form a triangle under the ching.

Austria: Crossed extended indexces.

England: Nose pressed upwards with thumb, tongue extruded.

France: Sticking out the tongue. Cheeks puffed out, left hand clenched against abdomen, right hand grasps nose, upper part of body doubled over. Customarily a mute gesture. Palm vertical, fingers extended and parted, thumb placed at tip of nose; thumb of other hand placed against tip of little fingers of first hand. Hand put over mouth, accompanied by mocking glances.

Germany: Hands placed to ears make waving movements, suggesting donkey's ears. Thumb to tip of nose, fingers extended.

Mexico: One finger of right hand extended and moved up and down as if playing a guitar. Index of right hand slides between angle of thumb and index of left hand, moving slowly as if playing a violing.

Netherlands: Hands raised to level of head, palms forward, fingers extended, thumbs placed in ears,tongue extruded. Mocking applause by tapping thumbnails together, one on top of the other.

Russia: Tip of extended index pushes up tip of nose which signifies mocker of someone who has a high opinion of himself or deems himself too good to do something.

Saudi Arabia: Tips of fingers and thumb joined and hitting on distended cheek, exhaling as fingers strike cheek. Can also signify that a given person is talking nonsense. Back of hand, fingers extended, placed beneath chin, fingers wiggling at someone regarded as old.

Spain: Thumb or index presses tip of nose upwards, fingers extended

Spain, Portugal: Right fist rubbed around on flat left hand.

U.S.: Crossing the eyes. Thumb or index presses tip of nose upwards, fingers extended

: A Functional Approach to Gestures

<u>MONEY</u>

Colombia: Forearm raised, palm forward, fingers repeatedly curled one after another or together. Palm facing person addressed, fingers move back and forth either together or one after the other.

Egypt, Lebanon, Jordan, Syria, Saudi Arabia: Tips of right index and thumb rub together, other fingers pressed into palm.

France: Movement of dropping money piece by piece between thumb and index; familiar. Rubbing thumb and index finger together.

Japan: Tips of thumb and index joined, forming a circle.

Korea: Index and thumb of right hand form a circle; remaining fingers are slightly spread open. Hand is held at waist height with palm facing stomach.

Latin America: Fist closed very loosely and the four fingertips then brush the palm inward several times. Rubbing the back of the thumb against the ball of the index finger. Extended fingertips of right hand brush up into the open left palm.

Mexico: Forearm extended, palm up, thumb and index from almost a complete circle, the remaining three fingers clenched upon palm.

Peru: Eyebrows raised to indicate "Pay me." Hand loosely open, edge of palm down, swept horizontally toward body as if sweeping something off a table.

Russia: Turning trouser pockets inside out

Spain, Latin America, Russia, Brazil: Accompanying expressions suggesting either possession or lack of money, thumb is rubbed over fingertips of same hand.

U.S.: Hand extended, palm up; request for money. Index and thumb of right hand form a circle; remaining fingers are slightly spread open. Hand is held at shoulder height with palm facing out.

PENSIVENESS

Africa: Head supported in the palm of the right hand, while the left hand holds the right elbow. Right hand moves as if gently pulling a beard. In a squatting position, the right hand drawing on the ground, the left hand, open, holding forehead. Right hand, thumb extended to the side, placed over mouth. With fixed expression, one moves the jaw and grinds the teeth.

Colombia: Thumb and index grasp chin. Thumb under chin, index along cheek. One hand grasps elbow or rests in armpit of the other, other hand against side of chin. Hands out to sides, fingers and thumbs of each hand rubbing together. Tips of fingers touch in front of or at lips or chin.

Germany: Index of left hand raised to mouth, lip pursed. Stroking the beard.

Netherlands: Tip of index placed at side of the nose.

Russia: Clasping the hands and nodding the head.

Saudi Arabia: Grasping chin with thumb side of right fist: sign of wisdom or maturity.

U.S.: Head cocked to one side, arms forward, fingers intertwined. Pulling one's ear. Drumming with fingers. Index or index and middle finger touch lower lip. Sometimes all fingers rest against lower lip. Palms rubbed together repeatedly as hands are firmly clasped. Fingers may be interlocked; indicates extreme concern.

PLEA

Africa: Squatting before someone and touching his feet; son pleading for forgiveness from his father. Right hand taps gently on left side of chest of the person whose pardon is sought.

France: Hands palm to palm, fingers of one hand interlaced with those of other, fingers of both hands bent down toward knuckles.

Italy: All fingers and thumb of right hand joined, the united tips pressed against forehead. Placing of hands together may be used in pleading or begging.

Netherlands: Hands clasped, fingers tightly interlocked, arms extended forward, kneeling.

Russia: Hands held vertically palm to palm below chin. If used by men or children it indicates a joking accompaniment to a plea or request.

Saudi Arabia: Placing right hand on beard or chin. Hands clasped in front of body, fingers tightly interlocked, then hands moved several times from the wrists: plea for mercy. Kissing the back of a dignitary's hand in plea for mercy.

Spain: Both arms extended in front of body, elbows close to side, palms facing one another. Joining palms of hand in front of the chest.

Spain, Latin America: Extending arms to side of gesticulator, palms up. Both arms extended in front of body, elbows close to side, palms facing one another.

U.S.: Flat hands, palm to palm, pointing toward a person.

REFUSAL

Africa: Right hand lightly slaps left forearm, which is raised so that the left hand faces the left shoulder. Both hand placed on nape of the neck, body turns brusquely to the side. Cheeks puffed up, mouth pointed forward. Tips of indexes placed in the ears. Index of right hand pulls down lower lie of right eye. Open hand, palm facing backwards, is moved backwards past one ear. Both hands open, raised to level of head and rotated inversely to each other in semi-circles backward and forward; indicates a solemn refusal.

Colombia: Arms crossed at wrist, palms facing forward; then hands move apart. Hands moved up and down, palms brushing each other.

France: Passing the index horizontally under the nose of another person, or one's own nose; familiar, but rarely used. One or both hands extended, palm facing forward. Flat hand, palm facing person addressed, describes arc by moving rapidly in front of chest from left to right or opposite direction.

India: Grasping one's earlobes signifies one's remorse.

Netherlands: Arms crossed on chest which indicates a refusal to be impressed or to participate. Tips of thumb placed in mouth, cheeks inflated. Open hand, vertical, raised to level of face, then dropped down from wrist.

Spain: Right hand, edge down, moves vertically downward, then, at right angle, horizontally from left to right.

Spain, Latin America: Shaking one hand, fingers slightly closed and palm outward at level of chest. Shaking index of one hand at or below the speaker's face.

U.S.: Eyes covered by hands.

REMINDER

Arab: Index or middle finger snapped on thumb. Putting right hand on someone's head, turning his ear with the left.

Argentina: Slapping forehead with extended fingers of right hand.

Colombia: Snapping fingers in an effort to remember something, or in the moment of remembering.

France: Sudden intuition or recall is expressed by fingertips of both hands slapping forehead sharply.

Germany: If one has overlooked or forgotten something, one should put the index finger into one's mouth, say "ff! ai! ai!," and make the sign of the cross.

Spain: Poking someone in the ribs with the elbow.

Spain, Latin America: Slapping the forehead with the fingers of one hand or with the base of the palm of the open hand.

U.S.: Tip of index touching forehead, then slowly pointed outward, palm facing in

REQUEST

Africa: Right arm raised, right hand open, or index pointing upwards to express "I want to speak." Both arms raised while snapping fingers of right hand. Both hands open, palm up, extended forward, or both hands open, palm up, extended forward, one hand crossed over the other. With simultaneous sign of regret, right hand extended toward someone, palm up, while left is placed on head. Right hand, palm down, clapped over lightly curled fingers of the left hand.

Colombia: Hand extended, palm up, fingers (except thumb) rapidly moving back and forth.

Netherlands: Hands vertical, palm to palm, under chin in a version of prayer gesture. Can be used in most banal or most dramatic circumstances, seriously or ironically. Striking one's bare head with the flat hand to signal to someone to take his hat off. Hands horizontal before face, index and middle finger extended and slightly apart, lips pursed in a request for a cigarette.

U.S.: Index pointing up or down is rotated to ask for another round of drinks.

RESPECT

Asia: Cross hands over stomach in an attitude of suffering as sign of utmost respect.

Brazil: Cessation of all activity in the presence of a superior. Placing hand over mouth in maintaining respectful silence.

China: Tapping with two fingers on a table. Bowing

Italy: Lowering eyes during prayer.

Japan: Turning one's back to someone.

Jordan, Kuwait, Saudi Arabia: Right fingertips touched to forehead while bowing head slightly.

Jordan, Lebanon, Saudi Arabia, Syria: Tips of right index touch mouth, second finger and thumb to mouth, bowing slightly.

Portugal: Women kneel on both knees, men on one.

Saudi Arabia: When greeting a dignitary, shake right hand, then the person of lower rank kisses own hand, places it on own chest and bows slightly. Stroking chin with fingers of right hand with downward motion. Kissing feet of a dignitary. Kissing a person's forehead, nose feet or right hand. Children kiss the top of their mother's head during Moslem holy days.

Saudi Arabia, Syria, Jordan, Lebanon, Kuwait, Iraq: Guests rise when an esteemed person enters house.

South Africa: Considered courteous to take the sandals off before entering the house of a stranger.

Tibet: Sticking out the tongue.

United Arab Emirates: Guests must take care not to rise while the host is sitting. The aim is never to stand higher than the host; if someone leaves, they bend while exiting, demonstrating a desire to stay lower. Physical demeanor is an outward sign of one's will and intent.

Vietnam: Listeners to someone speaking are expected to lower their eyes as sign of respect.

SHAME

Africa: Both hands over eyes. Tip of index of right placed between teeth, left hand covers eyes.

Europe: Shrinking, contracting of the body, bowing the head.

France: Fingers closed into fist, index and little finger raised and extended.

Jordan, Syria: Holding extended right thumb near chin with heel of hand out.

Saudi Arabia: Stroking chin with fingers of right hand with downward motion. Tip of right index place between eyebrows. May also be an admission of inability to do something.

U.S.: Lowering eyes and covering face with hands.

SILENCE

Africa: Elbow gives a neighboring person a blow in the side. Pressing lips together between teeth.

Arab: Biting lips, winking.

Colombia: Laying index vertically on lips. Thumb extended moves from one corner of closed lips to the other.

Egypt, Lebanon, Jordan, Saudi Arabia, Syria, Libya: One or both hands held before body with palms down, then moved slightly up and down several times.

France: Placing index over closed mouth. Tip of finger placed over closed mouth, index vertical.

Italy: Thumb and middle fingers in an open and closed motion while moving the hand away from the body.

Jordan, Kuwait, Lebanon, Libya, Saudi Arabia, Syria: Touching lower lip of a child with tip of right index.

Mexico: Lips pressed together with index and thumb of one hand.

Netherlands: To communicate a complaint about loud noise, person puts fingers into ears. Hand extended in front, waving up and down; demand for silence while telephoning.

Portugal: Putting index to nose.

Saudi Arabia: Gently grazing chin of another person with right fist; admonition not to argue. Placing extended right index in front of mouth and blowing on it.

Spain, Latin America: One or both outstretched hands, palms down, pushed toward the floor.

Spain, Portugal: Right hand, fingers extended and apart, palm up, moves gently up and down.

U.S.: Shutting lips with finger

Bibliography

Argyle,M(1975). *Bodily communication*. London:Metheun & Co. Ltd.
Argyle,M(1988). *Bodily communication*. London:Metheun & Co. Ltd.
Berko, R., Rosenfeld, L.,& Samovar, L .(1997). *Connecting: A culture-sensitive apoach to interpersonal communicative competency.* Orlando, FL:Harcourt Brace College Publishers.
Birdwhistell.R.L (1952) *Introduction to kinesics; An annontation system for analysis of body motion and gesture.* Ann Arbor, MI: University Microfilms.
Birdwhistell.R.L (1970). *Kineseics and context.* Philadelpha: University of Pennsylvania Press
Calloway-Thomas, C., Cooper. P & Blake, C. (1999). *Intercultural communication: Roots and routes.* Boston : Allyn and Bacon.
Collett, P (1971). On training Englishmen in the non-verbal behavior of Arads: An experiment in intercultural communication. *International; Joernal of Psychology*,6, 209-15
Darwin, C. (1872). *The expression of the emotions in man and animals.* London: John Murray
Davitz, J. R. (1964). *The communication of emotional meaning.* New York; Mc Graw Hill
Efron, D. (1941). *Gesture and and environment* . New York: King's Crown Press.
Ekman, P (1972). *Emotions in the human face*. Elmsford,NY: Pegamon Press
Ekman, P., &Friesen,W.V.(1975). *Unmasking in the face*. Englewood Cliffs,NJ PrenticeHall
Feldman, R.s.(Ed). (1982). *Development of nonverbal behavior in children.* New York; Springer-Verlag.
Gudykunst. W.,& Kim, Y.(1997). *Communicating with strangers: An approach to intercultural communication.* New York:McGraw-Hill Companies, Inc.
Hall, E.T.(1959) . *The silent language*. Garden City, NY: Doubleday.
Hargie, O. (1997). *A handbook of communication skills*. London: Routedge.
Knapp,M.,& Hall, J. (1997). *Nonverbal communication in the human interaction* Orlando, FL: Harcourt Brace College Publishers.
Knapp.M.L.,& Miller, G.R.(Eds.).(1985). *Handbook of interpersonal communication*. Beverly, CA:Sage
Kretschmer,E.(1925). *Psysique and character*. New York: Harcourt Brace Jovanovich.
Leathers,D.G(1997). *Successful nonverbal communication-Principies and applicartions. Boston: Allyn and Bacon*
Lewis, M.,& Rosenblum, L. A.(Eds.). (1978). *The development of affect.* New york: Pluenum.
Mehabian,A,(1972) *Nonverbal communication*. Chicago; Aldine-Atherton.
Meltzoff, A.N ., & Moore,M.K.(1983). Newborn infants imitate adult facial gestures.*Children Development, 54, 702-9*
Richmond, V., &McCroskey, J .(1995). *Nonverbal behavior in inertpersonal relations*. Boston; Alyn and Bacon.
Samovar, L.A& Porter, R.E.(1991). *Communication between cultures*. Belmont. CA: Wadworth
Sheldon,W.H.(1940) . *The Varieties of human physique*. New Yok: Harper Row.
Termine,N.T., & Izard, C.E.(1998). Infants' responses to their mother's expression of joy and sadness. *Develpmental Psychology*, 24,223-29.